TRIVQUIZ

1001

TRIVIA QUESTIONS

ARSENAL

FASCINATING FACTS! TRIVIA BRAINTEASERS!
WRITTEN AND ILLUSTRATED BY

DESIGNED BY JOE McGARRY

First published by Pitch Publishing, 2021

Pitch Publishing
A2 Yeoman Gate
Yeoman Way
Worthing
Sussex
BN13 3QZ
www.pitchpublishing.co.uk
info@pitchpublishing.co.uk

A CIP catalogue record is available for this book
from the British Library.

ISBN: 978 1 80150 013 5

Typesetting and origination by Pitch Publishing
Printed and bound in India by Replika Press Pvt. Ltd.

1001 TRIVIA QUESTIONS: ARSENAL

Other books in this series:

ACKNOWLEDGEMENTS

Thanks to Joe McGarry for his brilliant design work and his technical expertise. There would be no books without him!

Thanks to Debs McGarry for the research and art assistance.

Thanks to Luke McGarry for picking up the slack on the other features while we worked on this.

Thanks to all three for their patience!

Additional thanks to Tom and Andy at "Shoot! The Breeze" podcast and Rob Stokes for the additional research and scans!

ABOUT STEVE McGARRY

A former record sleeve designer, whose clients included Joy Division, Steve McGarry is one of the most prolific and widely-published cartoonists and illustrators that Britain has ever produced. In the UK alone, his national newspaper daily strips include "Badlands", which ran for a dozen years in The Sun, "The Diary of Rock & Pop" in the Daily Star, "Pop Culture" in Today and "World Soccer Diary" in The Sun.

Over his four-decade career he has regularly graced the pages of soccer magazines Match, Match of the Day and Shoot! and his comics work ranges from Romeo in the 1970s and Look-In, Tiger and Oink! in the 1980s, SI for Kids and FHM in the 1990s, through to the likes of Viz, MAD and Toxic! When The People launched his Steve McGarry's 20th Century Heroes series, they billed him as the world's top cartoonist.

His sports features have been published worldwide since 1982 and he currently has two features – "Biographic" and "Kid Town" – in newspaper syndication, with a client list that includes the New York Daily News and The Washington Post.

In recent years, he has also created story art for such movies as "Despicable Me 2", "The Minions" and "The Secret Life of Pets".

Although Manchester born and bred, Steve has been based in California since 1989. A two-term former President of the National Cartoonists Society, his honours include Illustrator of the Year awards from the NCS and the Australian Cartoonists Association, and he is a recipient of the prestigious Silver T-Square for "outstanding service to the profession of cartooning". In 2013, he was elected President of the NCS Foundation, the charitable arm of the National Cartoonists Society. He is also the founder and director of US comics festival NCSFest.

1001 QUESTIONS

THE FRENCH CONNECTION

IN HIS 22 YEARS AS **ARSENAL** MANAGER, FRENCHMAN **ARSENE WENGER** MADE 126 SIGNINGS ... AND 24 OF THOSE PLAYERS WERE ALSO FRENCH. SOME CAME FROM LEAGUES OTHER THAN FRANCE'S TOP FLIGHT -- **THIERRY HENRY** WAS SIGNED FROM **JUVENTUS**, FOR EXAMPLE -- BUT THE MAJORITY WERE SIGNED FROM A LIGUE 1 CLUB.

IDENTIFY THESE FRENCH PLAYERS SIGNED BY **WENGER:**

1 FULL-BACK SIGNED FROM **AUXERRE** IN 2007 FOR £7 MILLION, HE JOINED **MANCHESTER CITY** ON A FREE TRANSFER IN 2014, SHORTLY AFTER WINNING THE FA CUP.

2 SIGNED FROM **LORIENT** IN 2010, A CENTRE-BACK OF POLISH HERITAGE WHO WON THREE FA CUPS IN HIS NINE SEASONS WITH **ARSENAL** AND WAS CAPPED 51 TIMES BY **FRANCE**.

3 MIDFIELDER WHO HAD TWO SPELLS AT **ARSENAL** UNDER **WENGER**, EITHER SIDE OF FIVE SEASONS WITH **AC MILAN**, DURING WHICH HE WON A SERIE A TITLE. HE JOINED **CRYSTAL PALACE** IN 2016.

4 THE FIRST PLAYER TO JOIN **ARSENAL** FROM **MANCHESTER UNITED** SINCE **BRIAN KIDD** IN 1974, A FULL-BACK SIGNED IN 2008 AFTER NINE SEASONS AT OLD TRAFFORD THAT HAD SEEN HIM WIN FIVE PREMIER LEAGUE TITLES, THE UEFA CHAMPIONS LEAGUE, AN FA CUP, A LEAGUE CUP AND AN INTERCONTINENTAL CUP. HE MOVED ON TO **WERDER BREMEN** IN 2010.

5 CAPPED 84 TIMES BY **FRANCE**, A CENTRE-BACK WHO WON TWO PREMIER LEAGUE TITLES WITH **CHELSEA**, WAS AWARDED AND STRIPPED OF THE CAPTAINCY IN HIS FOUR SEASONS WITH **ARSENAL**, AND THEN JOINED **TOTTENHAM HOTSPUR** IN 2010.

6 CAPPED 21 TIMES BY **FRANCE** AND THREE TIMES BY **CORSICA**, CENTRE-BACK WHO HAD WON HONOURS WITH **AJACCIO, MONACO, LYON** AND **SEVILLA** PRIOR TO SPENDING THREE RELATIVELY UNHAPPY SEASONS WITH **THE GUNNERS** AFTER JOINING IN A £4 MILLION DEAL IN 2010.

7 DEFENSIVE MIDFIELDER SIGNED TO **ARSENAL** AS A TEEN, FOLLOWING LOAN SPELLS WITH **LORIENT**, **SC FREIBURG** AND **CHARLTON ATHLETIC**. HE WON TWO FA CUPS UNDER **WENGER** BEFORE JOINING **VILLARREAL**, WITH WHOM HE WON THE EUROPA LEAGUE IN 2020-21.

8 A TITLE WINNER WITH **MONACO**, HE JOINED **ARSENAL** IN 1997 AND WON A LEAGUE AND CUP DOUBLE IN HIS DEBUT SEASON. HE WON A SECOND DOUBLE IN HIS FINAL SEASON WITH **THE GUNNERS** BEFORE HEADING TO THE MLS. HE LATER SCOUTED FOR **ARSENAL**.

9 2001-02 FWA FOOTBALLER OF THE YEAR, A MIDFIELDER WHO WON THE 1998 WORLD CUP AND EURO 2000 WITH **FRANCE**, FOR WHOM HE WAS CAPPED 79 TIMES.

10 EURO 2000 WINNER CAPPED 92 TIMES BY **FRANCE**, A FORWARD WHO WON A LEAGUE TITLE WITH **BORDEAUX**, TWO PREMIER LEAGUES WITH **ARSENAL** AND THREE TITLES WITH **LYON**.

EURO HERO

19-YEAR-OLD **BUKAYO SAKA** WAS ONE OF THE STAND-OUT STARS FOR **ENGLAND** AT UEFA EURO 2020, WINNING THE MAN OF THE MATCH AWARD IN THE GROUP GAME AGAINST THE **CZECH REPUBLIC**. HIS TOURNAMENT ENDED IN SADNESS WHEN HE MISSED **ENGLAND'S** FIFTH PENALTY KICK IN THE SHOOTOUT THAT DECIDED THE FINAL TO GIVE **ITALY** THE CROWN.

OVER THE YEARS, A NUMBER OF PLAYERS -- INCLUDING THE LIKES OF **TONY ADAMS, DAVID SEAMAN, ALAN SMITH** AND **JACK WILSHERE** -- HAVE REPRESENTED **ENGLAND** IN A EUROPEAN CHAMPIONSHIP WHILE THEY WERE **ARSENAL** PLAYERS. NAME THE TEAMS THAT THE FOLLOWING WERE PLAYING WITH AT THE TIME OF THESE TOURNAMENTS:

1 1968: **ALAN BALL**

2 1980: **KENNY SANSOM**

3 1980: **TONY WOODCOCK**

4 1980: **VIV ANDERSON**

5 1980: **RAY KENNEDY**

6 1988: **VIV ANDERSON**

7 1992: **MARTIN KEOWN**

8 1992: **DAVID PLATT**

9 1996: **SOL CAMPBELL**

10 2000: **RICHARD WRIGHT**

11 2008: **ASHLEY COLE**

12 2008: **DANNY WELBECK**

THE BLUES BROTHERS

A PRODUCT OF THE YOUTH SYSTEM AT *ARSENAL*, *FABRICE MUAMBA* REPRESENTED *ENGLAND* AT ALL YOUTH LEVELS AND CAPTAINED THE UNDER-19 SIDE. HE ESTABLISHED HIS REPUTATION AS A DYNAMIC CENTRAL MIDFIELDER WITH *BIRMINGHAM CITY*, MOVING ON TO *BOLTON WANDERERS* IN 2008. DURING AN FA CUP GAME AGAINST *TOTTENHAM HOTSPUR* IN 2012, *FABRICE* SUFFERED A CARDIAC ARREST AND COLLAPSED. AFTER ATTEMPTS TO REVIVE HIM FAILED, THE GAME WAS ABANDONED, AND HE WAS RUSHED TO A NEARBY HOSPITAL. IT WAS LATER REVEALED THAT HIS HEART HAD STOPPED FOR 78 MINUTES. FORTUNATELY, HE RECOVERED -- BUT RETIRED FROM THE GAME ON MEDICAL ADVICE.

IDENTIFY THESE OTHERS WITH *ARSENAL* AND *BIRMINGHAM CITY* LINKS:

1 DOGGED BY INJURIES, CENTRAL DEFENDER WHO STRUGGLED TO BECOME A REGULAR AT *ARSENAL* -- DESPITE EARNING A PREMIER LEAGUE WINNER MEDAL IN 2002 -- HE PLAYED 21 TIMES FOR *ENGLAND* IN A CAREER THAT TOOK HIM TO *BIRMINGHAM CITY*, *WEST HAM*, *STOKE CITY*, *BRIGHTON & HOVE ALBION*, *LEICESTER CITY* AND MORE.

2 LEGENDARY *ARSENAL* GOALKEEPER WHOSE EARLY CLUBS INCLUDED *LEEDS UNITED*, *PETERBOROUGH UNITED* AND *BIRMINGHAM CITY*.

3 POWERFUL DANISH STRIKER WHO WAS LOANED OUT BY *ARSENAL* TO *BIRMINGHAM CITY*, *SUNDERLAND* AND *JUVENTUS* BEFORE JOINING *VFL WOLFSBURG* IN 2014 AFTER A DECADE WITH *THE GUNNERS*.

4 *POLAND* DEFENDER SIGNED FROM *LEGIA WARSAW* IN 2014, HE WAS LOANED OUT TO *BIRMINGHAM*, *WALSALL* AND *CHARLTON ATHLETIC* BEFORE JOINING *DERBY COUNTY* IN 2019.

5 FULL-BACK WHO, SHORTLY AFTER WINNING THE FA CUP IN 2014, HAD THE FIRST OF TWO LOANS WITH *WEST HAM*, FOLLOWED BY A LOAN PERIOD WITH *BIRMINGHAM CITY*, BEFORE SIGNING FOR *NOTTINGHAM FOREST* IN 2019.

6   *LIBERIA* STRIKER WHO PLAYED UNDER *ARSÈNE WENGER* AT *MONACO*, WON A LEAGUE AND FA CUP DOUBLE WITH *THE GUNNERS* IN 1998, SPENT TIME ON LOAN AT *AEK ATHENS*, *BIRMINGHAM CITY* AND *DEN BOSCH*, BEFORE HIS TRAVELS TOOK HIM TO TEAMS IN SCOTLAND, SAUDI ARABIA AND INDONESIA.

7   CAPPED 133 TIMES BY *SWEDEN*, HE WON A LEAGUE CUP WITH *BIRMINGHAM* AFTER LEAVING *ARSENAL* IN THE MID-2000S.

8   *ENGLAND* WINGER WHO RETIRED AT THE AGE OF 29 IN 2014 AFTER PLAYING FOR *ARSENAL*, *NORWICH CITY*, *BLACKBURN ROVERS*, *TOTTENHAM HOTSPUR*, *BIRMINGHAM CITY*, *WEST HAM UNITED* AND *FC ROSTOV*.

9   CAPPED 76 TIMES BY *SWITZERLAND*, CENTRAL DEFENDER WHO SPENT A DECADE WITH *ARSENAL*, DURING WHICH TIME HE SUFFERED A SUCCESSION OF INJURIES AND WAS LOANED OUT TO *BIRMINGHAM CITY* AND CLUBS IN GERMANY. HE LATER PLAYED IN GERMANY, TURKEY, ITALY AND DENMARK BEFORE RETIRING IN THE SUMMER OF 2021.

10   WAYWARD WINGER WHO MADE OVER 350 APPEARANCES FOR 15 CLUBS, HE LEFT *ARSENAL* FOR *BIRMINGHAM CITY* IN 2005 AND JOINED *LIVERPOOL* AFTER *THE BLUES* WERE RELEGATED.

EAGLES HAVE LANDED

MAROUANE CHAMAKH WAS BORN TO MOROCCAN PARENTS IN TONNEINS, FRANCE, ON JANUARY 10, 1984. HE ESTABLISHED HIS GOALSCORING PROWESS AT *BORDEAUX*, HELPING THE CLUB TO WIN A LEAGUE AND CUP DOUBLE IN 2009, BEFORE JOINING *ARSENAL* IN THE SUMMER OF 2010. DURING HIS THREE SEASONS WITH *THE GUNNERS* HE BECAME THE FIRST PLAYER TO SCORE IN SIX CONSECUTIVE EUROPEAN CHAMPIONS LEAGUE GAMES.

FOLLOWING A LOAN PERIOD AT *WEST HAM UNITED*, HE JOINED *CRYSTAL PALACE* IN 2013. IDENTIFY THESE OTHERS WHO ALSO PLAYED FOR BOTH *ARSENAL* AND *"THE EAGLES"*:

1   *ENGLAND* STRIKER WHO PLAYED FOR SIX LONDON CLUBS -- *QPR, ARSENAL, CRYSTAL PALACE, SPURS, WEST HAM* AND *MILLWALL* -- AS WELL AS *BORDEAUX, MANCHESTER CITY* AND MORE BETWEEN 1978 AND 1995.

2   *ENGLAND* STRIKER WHO IS *ARSENAL'S* SECOND-HIGHEST SCORER OF ALL TIME AND *CRYSTAL PALACE'S* THIRD-HIGHEST.

3   SCOTLAND STRIKER WHO LEFT *ARSENAL* IN 1996, HAD TWO SPELLS AT *MANCHESTER CITY*, TWO SPELLS AT *LEICESTER CITY* AND PLAYED FOR A NUMBER OF OTHER CLUBS, INCLUDING *CRYSTAL PALACE, BLACKBURN ROVERS* AND *LEEDS UNITED*.

4   *ENGLAND* FULL-BACK, WINNER OF PREMIER LEAGUE TITLES AND FA CUPS WITH *ARSENAL*, AND A PREMIER LEAGUE, CHAMPIONS LEAGUE, AND EUROPA LEAGUE WITH *CHELSEA*, WHO SPENT TIME ON LOAN AT *CRYSTAL PALACE* EARLY IN HIS CAREER.

5 ***REPUBLIC OF IRELAND*** WINGER WHO WAS PLAYER OF THE YEAR AT ***CRYSTAL PALACE***, WON A UEFA CUP WINNERS' CUP WITH ***ARSENAL*** IN 1994, MOVED ON TO ***MANCHESTER CITY*** AND BECAME A YOUTH TEAM COACH AT ***PALACE*** IN 2014.

6 ***ENGLAND'S*** SECOND MOST-CAPPED FULL-BACK WHO WAS TWICE ***CRYSTAL PALACE*** PLAYER OF THE YEAR, AND WON THE 1987 LEAGUE CUP AND WAS PLAYER OF THE YEAR AT ***ARSENAL***.

RED & WHITE DRAGONS

AN FA YOUTH CUP WINNER WITH **CRYSTAL PALACE**, **PETER NICHOLAS** HELPED THE CLUB WIN PROMOTION TO THE TOP FLIGHT IN 1979 BUT WAS SOLD TO **ARSENAL** SHORTLY BEFORE **THE EAGLES** SLIPPED BACK DOWN INTO THE SECOND TIER IN 1981. HE EARNED THE FIRST OF HIS 73 CAPS FOR **WALES** IN 1979 AND WENT ON TO CAPTAIN HIS COUNTRY.

1 *PETER NICHOLAS* MADE HIS *WALES* DEBUT IN MAY, 1979 AND PLAYED HIS LAST INTERNATIONAL IN NOVEMBER, 1991. NAME ONE OF THE FOUR *WALES* MANAGERS HE PLAYED UNDER.

2 BROTHER OF A *LEEDS UNITED* AND *JUVENTUS* LEGEND NICKNAMED *"THE GENTLE GIANT"*, WHICH VERSATILE *ARSENAL* PLAYER HAD REPRESENTED *WALES* AT THE 1958 WORLD CUP?

3 WHICH *WALES* STAR -- A MEMBER OF THE *GREAT BRITAIN* SQUAD AT THE 2012 OLYMPICS -- WON THREE FA CUPS WITH *ARSENAL* BEFORE SIGNING FOR *JUVENTUS* IN EARLY 2019?

4 A LEAGUE AND FA CUP WINNER WITH *ARSENAL*, WHICH *WALES* INTERNATIONAL MANAGED THE NATIONAL TEAM DURING THE FINAL TWO YEARS OF HIS PLAYING CAREER BETWEEN 1954 AND 1956?

5 STRIKER CAPPED 51 TIMES BY *WALES*, HE LEFT *ARSENAL* FOR *WEST HAM* IN EARLY 1997, WON MULTIPLE HONOURS WITH *CELTIC* AND SUCCESSFULLY BATTLED CANCER.

6 CAPTAIN OF *WALES* AT THE 1958 WORLD CUP, HE SPENT NINE YEARS WITH *ARSENAL*, SANDWICHED BETWEEN TWO SPELLS WITH *NORTHAMPTON TOWN*, THE TEAM HE WOULD LATER MANAGE TWICE. HE ALSO MANAGED *WALES* BETWEEN 1964 AND 1974.

7 JOURNEYMAN ENGLISH STRIKER WHO PLAYED FOR *ARSENAL* AND A NUMBER OF CLUBS BEFORE EMBARKING ON A MANAGEMENT CAREER THAT SAW HIM WIN THE 1988 FA CUP WITH *WIMBLEDON* AND SPEND FOUR YEARS MANAGING *WALES* IN THE LATE 1990S.

8 GOALKEEPING GREAT WHO WON THE LEAGUE WITH *ARSENAL* IN 1954 AND KEPT GOAL FOR *WALES* AT THE 1958 WORLD CUP.

BITING THE HAND THAT FED THEM ...

HAVING JOINED **ARSENAL** AT THE AGE OF 16, **SEBASTIAN LARSSON** HOVERED AROUND THE FRINGES OF THE SENIOR TEAM BEFORE A LOAN MOVE TO **BIRMINGHAM CITY** WAS MADE PERMANENT IN 2007. FOUR YEARS LATER, THE SWEDE RETURNED TO HAUNT **THE GUNNERS** WHEN HE PLAYED IN THE SIDE THAT BEAT **ARSENAL** IN THE 2011 LEAGUE CUP FINAL.

IDENTIFY THESE OTHER FORMER **GUNNERS** WHO TORMENTED **ARSENAL:**

1 FOLLOWING AN ACRIMONIOUS TRANSFER TO **MANCHESTER CITY** IN THE SUMMER OF 2019, WHICH PLAYER REACTED TO ABUSE FROM THE AWAY END BY RACING THE FULL LENGTH OF THE ETIHAD PITCH TO CELEBRATE HIS GOAL IN FRONT OF THE **ARSENAL** FANS, RECEIVING A BOOKING FOR HIS EFFORTS?

2 HAVING BEEN SOLD TO **BARCELONA** IN 2003, WHICH PLAYER RETURNED TO HAUNT **ARSENAL** WHEN HE PLAYED IN THE SIDE THAT BEAT **THE GUNNERS** IN THE 2006 CHAMPIONS LEAGUE FINAL?

3 WHICH FORMER **ARSENAL** PLAYER SCORED THE WINNING GOAL AGAINST **TOTTENHAM HOTSPUR** ON THE FINAL DAY OF THE SEASON THAT MEANT **MANCHESTER UNITED** FINISHED ONE POINT ABOVE **THE GUNNERS** TO WIN THE PREMIER LEAGUE IN 1999?

4 WHICH FORMER **ARSENAL** HERO WAS A MEMBER OF THE 2012 CHAMPIONS-ELECT SIDE GIVEN A GUARD OF HONOUR AT **THE EMIRATES** WHEN HE RETURNED THE SEASON AFTER LEAVING **THE GUNNERS** -- RUBBING SALT IN TO THE WOUND BY SCORING?

5 WHICH **ARSENAL** CAPTAIN, HAVING REJOINED HIS BOYHOOD CLUB OF **BARCELONA**, RETURNED TO LONDON IN 2014 -- AND STUNNED **ARSENAL** FANS BY SIGNING FOR **CHELSEA?**

6 WHICH FORMER **ARSENAL** MANAGER BROKE **ARSENAL** HEARTS WHEN HE GUIDED **VILLARREAL** TO VICTORY OVER **THE GUNNERS** IN A UEFA EUROPA LEAGUE SEMI-FINAL?

7 WHICH FORMER *ARSENAL* BOSS MANAGED *TOTTENHAM HOTSPUR* TO A 2-1 VICTORY OVER *THE GUNNERS* AT *WHITE HART LANE* IN 1999?

8 WHICH FORMER *ARSENAL* STRIKER SCORED IN A 4-1 WIN FOR *CHELSEA* IN 2009 THAT SECURED AUTOMATIC UEFA CHAMPIONS LEAGUE QUALIFICATION FOR THE BLUES AND CONDEMNED *ARSENAL* TO FOURTH PLACE?

"MR. ARSENAL"

CAPPED 66 TIMES BY *ENGLAND*, *TONY ADAMS* SPENT HIS ENTIRE PLAYING CAREER WITH *ARSENAL*. HE WON FOUR TOP FLIGHT DIVISION TITLES -- CAPTAINING A TITLE-WINNING TEAM IN THREE DIFFERENT DECADES -- THREE FA CUPS, TWO FOOTBALL LEAGUE CUPS AND A UEFA CUP WINNERS' CUP BEFORE RETIRING IN 2002. A RUGGED CENTRAL DEFENDER, *ADAMS* WAS THE FIRST *ENGLAND* PLAYER TO MAKE TOURNAMENT APPEARANCES IN THREE SEPARATE DECADES.

1 NAME THE EIGHT MANAGERS UNDER WHOM *TONY ADAMS* PLAYED AT *ARSENAL*.

2 WHO GAVE *ADAMS* HIS *ENGLAND* DEBUT IN 1987?

3 WHICH *ENGLAND* MANAGER STRIPPED *ADAMS* OF THE CAPTAINCY AND AWARDED IT TO *ALAN SHEARER?*

4 WHICH MANAGER RE-INSTATED *ADAMS* AS CAPTAIN FOLLOWING *SHEARER'S ENGLAND* RETIREMENT AFTER EURO 2000?

5 *ADAMS* CAPTAINED *ENGLAND* 15 TIMES -- WHICH *ARSENAL* PLAYER CAPTAINED *ENGLAND* 19 TIMES BETWEEN 1993 AND 1995?

6 HIS FIRST JOB IN MANAGEMENT WAS AT WHICH CLUB WHO, COINCIDENTALLY, PLAY HOME GAMES AT *ADAMS PARK?*

7 HAVING ASSISTED *HARRY REDKNAPP* AT THE CLUB, *ADAMS* WAS APPOINTED MANAGER OF WHICH TEAM IN 2008?

8 *TONY ADAMS* WAS APPOINTED MANAGER, AND LATER SPORTING DIRECTOR, OF *GABALA* -- A CLUB BASED IN WHICH COUNTRY?

9 HE WAS SACKED, AFTER LOSING ALL SEVEN GAMES IN CHARGE, BY WHICH LA LIGA CLUB IN 2017?

10 WHAT WAS HIS SHIRT NUMBER AT *ARSENAL?*

THE BOYS OF 1994

ON MAY 4, 1994, A SINGLE GOAL FROM **ALAN "SMUDGE" SMITH** WAS ENOUGH TO SEAL VICTORY OVER **PARMA** AND MAKE **GEORGE GRAHAM'S ARSENAL** THE FOURTH LONDON CLUB -- AFTER **TOTTENHAM HOTSPUR, CHELSEA** AND **WEST HAM UNITED** -- TO WIN THE EUROPEAN CUP WINNERS' CUP.

CAN YOU NAME THE CLUB THAT EACH MEMBER OF THAT CUP-WINNING TEAM JOINED AFTER LEAVING **ARSENAL** *(OR IF THEY SUBSEQUENTLY RETIRED FROM PLAYING WHEN THEIR **ARSENAL** CAREER ENDED)?*

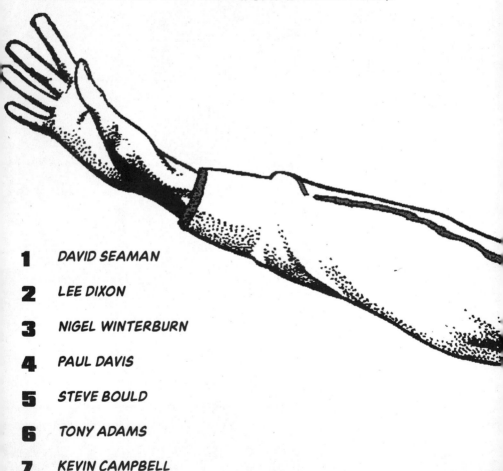

1   *DAVID SEAMAN*

2   *LEE DIXON*

3   *NIGEL WINTERBURN*

4   *PAUL DAVIS*

5   *STEVE BOULD*

6   *TONY ADAMS*

7   *KEVIN CAMPBELL*

8   *STEVE MORROW*

9 ALAN SMITH

10 PAUL MERSON

11 IAN SELLEY

12 ANDY LINIGHAN

13 ALAN MILLER

14 EDDIE McGOLDRICK

15 RAY PARLOUR

16 PAUL DICKOV

THE RUSSIANS ARE COMING!

HAVING WON MULTIPLE HONOURS IN HIS NATIVE RUSSIA WITH *ZENIT SAINT PETERSBURG* -- INCLUDING LEAGUE, CUP AND UEFA CUP -- *ANDREY ARSHAVIN* JOINED *ARSENAL* IN EARLY 2009, THE £15 MILLION TRANSFER FEE MAKING HIM THE CLUB'S MOST EXPENSIVE SIGNING AT THE TIME. A FORMER RUSSIAN PLAYER OF THE YEAR, HE JOINED *ARSENAL* ON THE BACK OF HIS OUTSTANDING DISPLAYS AT EURO 2008 AND ALTHOUGH HE MADE AN IMPRESSIVE START TO HIS TIME IN ENGLAND, HIS FORM TAILED OFF AND HE RETURNED TO *ZENIT SAINT PETERSBURG* ON LOAN IN 2012, THE MOVE BECOMING PERMANENT THE FOLLOWING YEAR.

THE FOLLOWING HAVE LINKS TO *ARSENAL* AND RUSSIAN TEAMS:

1 SIX-TIMES BELARUSSIAN FOOTBALLER OF THE YEAR, AN ATTACKING MIDFIELDER WHO WAS ON THE LOSING SIDE IN THE 2006 UEFA CHAMPIONS LEAGUE FINAL AND 2007 LEAGUE CUP FINAL, HE SPENT AN UNHAPPY TIME AT *BARCELONA* BEFORE JOINING THE RUSSIAN PREMIER LEAGUE'S *KRYLIA SOVETOV SAMARA* IN EARLY 2012.

2 GHANAIAN MIDFIELDER WHOSE CAREER TOOK HIM FROM *ARSENAL* TO *BARNSLEY* VIA LOAN SPELLS AT *WOLVES, CHARLTON* AND *FULHAM*, BEFORE JOINING RUSSIAN TEAM *UFA* IN 2014.

3 *ENGLAND* WINGER -- DUBBED THE *"NEW DAVID BECKHAM"* -- WHO LAUNCHED HIS CAREER AT *ARSENAL* AND PLAYED FOR A NUMBER OF CLUBS, INCLUDING *NORWICH CITY, BLACKBURN ROVERS, TOTTENHAM HOTSPUR, WEST HAM, BIRMINGHAM CITY* AND RUSSIA'S *FC ROSTOV* BEFORE BECOMING DISILLUSIONED AND HANGING UP HIS BOOTS AGED 29.

4 CAPPED 131 TIMES BY *SWEDEN*, HE WON TWO LEAGUE TITLES WITH *LYON* BEFORE EARNING AN FA CUP MEDAL WITH *ARSENAL* IN 2014 WHILE ON LOAN FROM *SPARTAK MOSCOW*.

5 SUBSEQUENT MANAGER OF *ARSENAL* WHO SPENT SIX MONTHS IN CHARGE OF *SPARTAK MOSCOW* IN 2012.

6 DUTCH-BORN *GHANA* INTERNATIONAL LEFT *ARSENAL* FOR *SPARTAK MOSCOW* IN 2006 AND WENT ON TO PLAY IN SPAIN WITH *CELTA VIGO* AND *MÁLAGA*, PLAY FOR *BIRMINGHAM CITY*, *CARDIFF CITY* AND *PORTSMOUTH*, *AL-SADD* OF QATAR, GREEK CLUB *PANATHINAIKOS*, *BOAVISTA* OF PORTUGAL, AND IN HIS NATIVE NETHERLANDS WITH *NEC* AND *SV ROBINHOOD*.

7 *CAMEROON* INTERNATIONAL WHOSE *ARSENAL* PERFORMANCES EARNED HIM A TRANSFER TO *BARCELONA* IN 2012, HE HAD TWO SEASONS ON LOAN AT *WEST HAM* AND SUBSEQUENTLY PLAYED FOR RUSSIA'S *RUBIN KAZAN*, SWITZERLAND'S *SION* AND IN DJIBOUTI WITH *AS ARTA/SOLAR7*.

GUNNERS AND HAMMERS

AFTER LEARNING HIS TRADE AT YOUTH LEVEL WITH A NUMBER OF CLUBS IN HIS NATIVE POLAND, **LUKASZ FABIANSKI** SIGNED PROFESSIONAL TERMS WITH **LECH POZNAŃ** AT THE AGE OF 19, MOVING ON TO **LEGIA WARSAW** THE FOLLOWING YEAR. **FABIANSKI** FIRST REPRESENTED HIS COUNTRY AT U-15 LEVEL AND PROGRESSED THROUGH THE JUNIOR RANKS BEFORE WINNING HIS FIRST FULL CAP IN 2006. HE WON THE FA CUP WITH ARSENAL IN 2014, WAS VOTED PLAYER OF THE YEAR AT SWANSEA CITY AND HAMMER OF THE YEAR IN HIS DEBUT SEASON FOR WEST HAM UNITED.

IDENTIFY THESE OTHER PLAYERS WITH LINKS TO **THE GUNNERS** AND **THE HAMMERS:**

1 SPANISH GOALKEEPER WHO WON THE FA CUP WITH **ARSENAL** IN 2004, HE SPENT A SEASON ON LOAN WITH **WEST HAM** BEFORE JOINING **WATFORD** IN 2012.

2 FRENCH STRIKER CAPPED 13 TIMES BY **GUINEA**, HE PLAYED FOR **ARSENAL** IN 1999, SPENT TIME WITH **BLACKBURN ROVERS** AND **WEST HAM UNITED** AND PLAYED IN FRANCE, SPAIN AND TURKEY.

3 PORTUGUESE MIDFIELDER WHO WON THE PREMIER LEAGUE WITH **ARSENAL** IN 1998, JOINED **SOUTHAMPTON** AND WON A FIRST DIVISION TITLE WITH **FULHAM**, BEFORE SPENDING FIVE SEASONS AT **WEST HAM**. HE LATER PLAYED IN GREECE AND THE STATES BEFORE ENDING HIS PLAYING DAYS WITH **CHESTERFIELD**.

4 FRENCH STRIKER WHO WON A PREMIER LEAGUE MEDAL WITH **ARSENAL** IN 2004 BEFORE LOAN SPELLS WITH **CELTIC**, **WEST HAM** AND **WOLVES**. HE SPENT THREE SEASONS WITH **MIDDLESBROUGH** BEFORE PLAYING IN FRANCE AND QATAR.

5 **ARSENAL'S** FOURTH-HIGHEST GOALSCORER OF ALL TIME, HE WON A LEAGUE AND FA CUP WITH **THE GUNNERS** IN 1971, AND LATER PLAYED FOR **WEST HAM UNITED, BLACKBURN ROVERS** AND **BISHOP'S STORTFORD**.

6 1998 FIFA WORLD CUP GOLDEN BOOT WINNER, HIS CLUBS INCLUDED **ARSENAL, WEST HAM, SEVILLA** AND **REAL MADRID**.

7 ISRAELI MIDFIELDER
WHOSE CLUBS
INCLUDED
ARSENAL,
WEST HAM,
LIVERPOOL,
CHELSEA
AND **QPR.**

THE YOUNG ONES

WHEN **CESC FÀBREGAS** MADE HIS SENIOR DEBUT AGAINST **ROTHERHAM UNITED** IN A LEAGUE CUP THIRD ROUND GAME IN OCTOBER 2003, HE BECAME -- AT THE AGE OF 16 YEARS AND 177 DAYS -- **ARSENAL'S** YOUNGEST-EVER FIRST-TEAM PLAYER. A FEW WEEKS LATER, WHEN HE NETTED AGAINST **WOLVERHAMPTON WANDERERS** IN THE FOURTH ROUND OF THE COMPETITION AT THE AGE OF 16 YEARS AND 212 DAYS, HE BECAME THE CLUB'S YOUNGEST-EVER GOALSCORER.

IDENTIFY THESE OTHER FRESH-FACED **ARSENAL** YOUNGSTERS:

1 **ARSENAL'S** YOUNGEST-EVER LEAGUE PLAYER WHEN HE MADE HIS DEBUT, AT THE AGE OF 16 YEARS AND 256 DAYS, AGAINST **BLACKBURN ROVERS** IN 2008. HE WENT ON TO WIN 34 **ENGLAND** CAPS AND PLAY FOR **WEST HAM UNITED** AND **BOURNEMOUTH**.

2 WINGER WHO MADE HIS DEBUT AGED 16 YEARS AND 319 DAYS AGAINST **MIDDLESBROUGH** IN THE LEAGUE CUP IN NOVEMBER, 1999 -- BUT HAD TO WAIT ANOTHER TWO-AND-A-HALF YEARS FOR HIS LEAGUE DEBUT! HIS SUBSEQUENT CLUBS INCLUDED **LIVERPOOL**, **REAL ZARAGOZA** AND **STOKE CITY**.

3 HAVING MADE HIS SENIOR DEBUT AGED 16 YEARS AND 346 DAYS AGAINST **LOKOMOTIVE LEIPZIG** IN THE UEFA CUP IN 1978, HE SCORED THE GOAL AGAINST **JUVENTUS** THAT PUT **THE GUNNERS** IN THE 1980 EUROPEAN CUP WINNERS' CUP FINAL. INJURY ENDED HIS CAREER BEFORE HE REACHED HIS 21ST BIRTHDAY.

4 LEFT-WINGER WHO MADE HIS DEBUT AGAINST **HUDDERSFIELD TOWN** IN 1953 AT THE AGE OF 16 YEARS AND 321 DAYS TO BECOME **ARSENAL'S** YOUNGEST-EVER LEAGUE DEBUTANT, A RECORD THAT STOOD FOR 55 YEARS.

5 **ENGLAND** STAR WHO BECAME THE FIRST PLAYER BORN IN THE 21ST CENTURY TO PLAY IN A PREMIER LEAGUE MATCH FOR **ARSENAL** WHEN HE APPEARED AGAINST **FULHAM** IN EARLY 2019.

6 **DENMARK** STRIKER WHO DEBUTED AGED 17 IN 2005.

7 **CARDIFF CITY** PRODIGY WHO PLAYED IN AN FA CUP FINAL BEFORE JOINING **ARSENAL** AND MAKING HIS DEBUT AGED 17 IN 2008.

8 **ARSENAL'S** YOUNGEST-EVER HAT-TRICK SCORER, AGAINST **WOLVES** IN JANUARY 1965, AT THE AGE OF 17 YEARS AND 315 DAYS.

POKAL POWER!

IN EARLY 2008, AFTER JUST 37 APPEARANCES FOR *FC SCHALKE 04*, *MESUT ÖZIL* BECAME THE MOST EXPENSIVE TEENAGER IN GERMAN FOOTBALL HISTORY WHEN HE SIGNED FOR *WERDER BREMEN*. HE HELPED *BREMEN* FINISH RUNNERS-UP IN THE LEAGUE THAT FIRST SEASON, REACH THE FINAL OF THE UEFA CUP AND WIN THE DFB-POKAL CUP, *MESUT* SCORING THE ONLY GOAL IN A 1-0 VICTORY OVER *BAYER LEVERKUSEN.*

THE FOLLOWING *ARSENAL* PLAYERS REPRESENTED WHICH CLUB IN A DFB-POKAL CUP FINAL?

1 2008: *LUKAS PODOLSKI*

2 2010: *PER MERTESACKER*

3 2015: *NICKLAS BENDTNER*

4 2016: *SOKRATIS PAPASTATHOPOULOS*

5 2017: *PIERRE-EMERICK AUBAMEYANG*

6 2019: *SERGE GNABRY*

GOING DUTCH

ROBIN VAN PERSIE MADE HIS DEBUT FOR FEYENOORD AT THE AGE OF 17. DESPITE BEING A MEMBER OF THE TEAM THAT WON THE 2002 UEFA CUP, HIS CLASHES WITH COACH BERT VAN MARWIJK SAW HIM INCREASINGLY SIDELINED. HE JOINED ARSENAL IN 2004 AND IN HIS EIGHT SEASONS WITH THE CLUB, WON AN FA CUP AND A PREMIER LEAGUE GOLDEN BOOT.

IDENTIFY THESE OTHER ARSENAL PLAYERS WITH DUTCH LINKS:

1   VAN PERSIE WAS SIGNED AS A LONG-TERM REPLACEMENT FOR WHICH DUTCH SUPERSTAR WHO WON THREE PREMIER LEAGUE TITLES AND FOUR FA CUP TROPHIES WITH THE GUNNERS?

2   CAPPED 106 TIMES BY THE NETHERLANDS, WHOM HE CAPTAINED IN THE 2010 WORLD CUP FINAL, HE WON LEAGUE AND CUP HONOURS WITH ARSENAL AND RANGERS, LEAGUE, CUP AND CHAMPIONS LEAGUE WITH BARCELONA, AND WON LEAGUE TITLES WITH FEYENOORD IN BOTH HIS PLAYING DAYS AND AS A MANAGER.

3   GEORGE GRAHAM'S LAST SIGNING, HE ARRIVED FROM VITESSE ARNHEM AND WAS LOANED TO BENFICA BY ARSÈNE WENGER.

4   THE ORIGINAL "FLYING DUTCHMAN", HE KEPT GOAL IN THE SIDE THAT WON ARSENAL'S FIRST TOP FLIGHT TITLE IN 1931.

5   BELGIAN CENTRAL DEFENDER WHO WON LEAGUE AND CUP HONOURS WITH AJAX, THE 2014 FA CUP WITH ARSENAL AND MULTIPLE HONOURS WITH BARCELONA, INCLUDING FOUR LEAGUE TITLES, THE UEFA CHAMPIONS LEAGUE AND FIFA CLUB WORLD CUP.

6   JAPANESE WINGER WHOSE FOUR YEARS WITH ARSENAL WERE SPENT MAINLY ON LOAN WITH BOLTON WANDERERS AND WIGAN ATHLETIC AND DUTCH CLUBS FEYENOORD AND FC TWENTE.

7   FRENCH STRIKER SIGNED FROM AUXERRE, HE HAD LOAN SPELLS WITH CRYSTAL PALACE, CHARLTON ATHLETIC AND AJAX, JOINED TOULOUSE IN 2017 AND HUDDERSFIELD TOWN IN 2021.

8   LEAGUE, CUP AND CHAMPIONS LEAGUE WINNER WITH AJAX, HE WON THE DOUBLE WITH ARSENAL IN 1998 BEFORE HIS £25 MILLION TRANSFER TO BARCELONA MADE THE WINGER THE MOST EXPENSIVE PLAYER IN DUTCH FOOTBALL HISTORY TO THAT POINT.

SAINTLY BOYS

WHEN 16-YEAR-OLD *THEO WALCOTT* MADE HIS SENIOR DEBUT FOR *HARRY REDKNAPP'S SOUTHAMPTON* ON THE FIRST DAY OF THE 2005-06 SEASON, HE BECAME THE CLUB'S YOUNGEST-EVER PLAYER TO THAT POINT -- AND COMPLETED ONE OF FOOTBALL'S MOST METEORIC RISES! BORN IN THE STANMORE AREA OF LONDON AND RAISED IN A SMALL VILLAGE NEAR NEWBURY, BERKSHIRE, HE HADN'T EVEN PLAYED FOOTBALL UNTIL HE WAS 10 YEARS OLD! HE WAS SNAPPED UP BY *ARSENAL* TWO MONTHS BEFORE HIS 17TH BIRTHDAY, AND LATER THAT YEAR, THE FOOTBALL WORLD WAS STUNNED WHEN HE WAS INCLUDED IN *ENGLAND'S* WORLD CUP SQUAD -- BEFORE HE HAD EVEN PLAYED FOR *ARSENAL'S* FIRST TEAM! IN HIS SECOND INTERNATIONAL APPEARANCE, *WALCOTT* BECAME THE YOUNGEST PLAYER TO SCORE A HAT-TRICK FOR *ENGLAND*.

IDENTIFY THESE *GUNNERS* WITH *SOUTHAMPTON* LINKS:

1 A RECORD £220,000 TRANSFER FROM *EVERTON* TO *ARSENAL* IN 1971, HE HAD TWO SPELLS AS A PLAYER WITH *SOUTHAMPTON* AND LATER STEERED THE CLUB AWAY FROM RELEGATION AS MANAGER.

2 A TEEN STAR WITH *SOUTHAMPTON*, HE JOINED *ARSENAL* IN 2011, WITH WHOM HE WON THREE FA CUPS IN SEVEN SEASONS BEFORE SIGNING FOR *LIVERPOOL* IN 2017.

3 A LEAGUE AND FA CUP DOUBLE WINNER IN 1971, HE HAD TWO SPELLS WITH *DERBY COUNTY* AND PLAYED FOR *SOUTHAMPTON* AND CLUBS IN THE STATES, HONG KONG, SCOTLAND AND ENGLAND.

4 CAPPED SIX TIMES BY *ENGLAND*, HE REACHED THE 1979 LEAGUE CUP FINAL WITH *SOUTHAMPTON*, WON THE 1987 LEAGUE CUP WITH *ARSENAL*, MOVING ON TO *LUTON TOWN* A YEAR LATER.

5 SIGNED FROM *SOUTHAMPTON* IN 2014, HIS TIME AT *ARSENAL* HAS INCLUDED LOAN SPELLS AT *MIDDLESBROUGH*, AND AT *FULHAM*, WHERE HE WAS VOTED 2018-19 PLAYER OF THE SEASON.

6 *WALES* INTERNATIONAL AND SUBSEQUENT MANAGER OF THE NATIONAL TEAM, HE WON LEAGUE AND FA CUP HONOURS WITH *ARSENAL* AFTER LEAVING *SOUTHAMPTON* IN 1943.

7 **GEORGE GRAHAM'S** FIRST SIGNING FOR **ARSENAL** WHEN TRANSFERRED FROM **COLCHESTER UNITED**, HE WON TWO LEAGUE TITLES AND A LEAGUE CUP BEFORE JOINING **SOUTHAMPTON** IN 1992, WHERE HIS CAREER WAS CURTAILED BY INJURY.

8 HIS GOALSCORING PROWESS CONVINCED **ARSENAL** TO SIGN HIM FROM **SOUTHAMPTON** IN 1934 AND THEY WERE REWARDED WITH TWO LEAGUE TITLES AND AN FA CUP. HE LATER MANAGED **CHELSEA** TO THE LEAGUE TITLE IN 1955.

9 PORTUGUESE INTERNATIONAL WHO SPENT FIVE SEASONS WITH **SOUTHAMPTON** AND JOINED **ARSENAL** IN 2020 AFTER A LOAN SPELL WITH **INTERNAZIONALE**.

10 SIGNED BY **ARSÈNE WENGER** IN 1997, A PORTUGUESE INTERNATIONAL WHO MOVED ON TO **SOUTHAMPTON** BEFORE BECOMING AN INSPIRATIONAL CAPTAIN OF **FULHAM** AND LATER PLAYING FOR FIVE SEASONS AT **WEST HAM**.

PÉPÉ LE WHOO!!!

SON OF A PRISON GUARD, **NICOLAS PÉPÉ** PLAYED IN GOAL UNTIL HE WAS 14 YEARS OLD. THE SWITCH TO AN OUTFIELD POSITION PAID OFF -- HE SIGNED TO **ARSENAL** FOR A CLUB RECORD £72 MILLION FEE IN THE SUMMER OF 2019, WINNING THE FA CUP IN HIS DEBUT SEASON!

1 HAVING LAUNCHED HIS CAREER WITH **POITIERS** AND **ANGERS**, HE JOINED WHICH LIGUE 1 CLUB IN 2017, WHERE HE PLAYED UNDER HEAD COACH **MARCELO BIELSA?**

2 ALTHOUGH BORN IN FRANCE, **PÉPÉ** PLAYS HIS INTERNATIONAL FOOTBALL FOR WHICH COUNTRY?

3 WHILE PLAYING IN FRANCE, **PÉPÉ** WON THE PRIX MARC-VIVIEN FOÉ, AN AWARD GIVEN TO THE BEST AFRICAN PLAYER IN LIGUE 1. NAME THE THREE OTHER PLAYERS WHO WOULD LATER PLAY FOR **ARSENAL** WHO ALSO WON THE AWARD:
A) **MOROCCO** STRIKER WHO WON THE AWARD IN 2009 WHILE PLAYING FOR **BORDEAUX;**
B) **IVORY COAST** STAR WHO WON THE AWARD IN 2011 AND 2012 WHILE PLAYING FOR **LILLE;**
C) **GABON** STRIKER WHO WON THE AWARD WITH **SAINT-ÉTIENNE** BEFORE HIS MOVE TO **BORUSSIA DORTMUND.**

4 **PÉPÉ'S** TRANSFER FEE TO **ARSENAL** IN 2019 ECLIPSED THE CLUB RECORD OF £56 MILLION SET A YEAR EARLIER WHEN **THE GUNNERS** SIGNED WHICH STRIKER?

5 WHO WAS THE MANAGER WHO SIGNED HIM TO **ARSENAL?**

6 ON ARRIVAL AT **ARSENAL**, HE TOOK WHICH SHIRT NUMBER PREVIOUSLY WORN BY GOALKEEPER **BERND LENO?**

7 HE SCORED HIS FIRST **ARSENAL** GOAL, FROM THE PENALTY SPOT, IN A 3-2 HOME WIN OVER WHICH TEAM IN SEPTEMBER, 2019?

8 HE RECEIVED THE FIRST RED CARD OF HIS CAREER WHEN HE WAS SENT OFF FOR HEADBUTTING WHICH **LEEDS UNITED** PLAYER?

WORKING FOR THE MAN!

NICOLAS ANELKA WAS ONCE BANNED FOR FIVE MATCHES BY THE FA AND FINED £80,000 AFTER MAKING AN OFFENSIVE HAND GESTURE, CALLED THE **"QUENELLE"**, THAT FRENCH AUTHORITIES HAVE SOUGHT TO BAN. HE WAS CAPPED 69 TIMES BY **FRANCE** BUT HIS INTERNATIONAL CAREER GROUND TO A HALT WHEN HE WAS EXPELLED FROM THE SQUAD AFTER INSULTING MANAGER **RAYMOND DOMENECH** AT HALF-TIME IN A 2010 WORLD CUP GAME AGAINST **MEXICO**.

ANELKA PLAYED UNDER THE FOLLOWING MANAGERS FOR WHICH TEAMS?

1   *VICENTE DEL BOSQUE*

2   *KEVIN KEEGAN*

3   *SAM ALLARDYCE*

4   *JOHN TOSHACK*

5   *AVRAM GRANT*

6   *GARY MEGSON*

7   *JEAN TIGANA*

8   *GÉRARD HOULLIER*

9   *GUUS HIDDINK*

10 *PETER REID*

11 *PEPE MEL*

12 *LUIS FERNANDEZ*

13 *ZICO*

14 *ANDRÉ VILLAS-BOAS*

THE HORNETS' NEST

WHEN **ARSENAL** HIJACKED **PARK CHU-YOUNG'S** 2011 MOVE FROM **MONACO** TO **LILLE**, THE 26-YEAR-OLD WAS CAPTAIN OF **SOUTH KOREA**. BY THE TIME HE LEFT **THE GUNNERS** IN 2014, HAVING MADE JUST SEVEN APPEARANCES, HE HAD LOST THE ARMBAND, HIS PLACE IN THE NATIONAL SIDE AND HIS EUROPEAN ADVENTURE WAS OVER. BY 2015, HE WAS BACK AT **FC SEOUL**, THE CLUB WHERE HE LAUNCHED HIS CAREER.

PARK CHU-YOUNG HAD A BRIEF PERIOD ON LOAN AT **WATFORD** -- IDENTIFY THESE OTHER PLAYERS WITH LINKS TO **THE HORNETS:**

1   SIX-TIME ESTONIAN PLAYER OF THE YEAR KEPT GOAL FOR **DERBY COUNTY**, **SUNDERLAND**, **ARSENAL**, **WATFORD** AND MORE.

2   PACEY SPANISH RIGHT-BACK WHO RETURNED FROM A LOAN SPELL WITH **WATFORD** IN 2014 AND WENT ON TO WIN THREE FA CUPS.

3   **NORTHERN IRELAND** GOALKEEPER WHO STARTED HIS CAREER IN ENGLAND WITH **WATFORD** AND WENT ON TO WIN FA CUPS WITH **ARSENAL** AND **TOTTENHAM HOTSPUR**.

4   AFTER WINNING THE FA CUP WITH **IPSWICH TOWN** IN 1978, HE JOINED **ARSENAL** AND WON IT AGAIN IN 1979 -- THE FIRST PLAYER FOR MORE THAN 100 YEARS TO WIN THE FA CUP WITH TWO DIFFERENT TEAMS IN CONSECUTIVE SEASONS. SUBSEQUENT CLUBS INCLUDED **WATFORD**, **STOKE CITY**, **WEST BROM** AND **FULHAM**.

5   **NORTHERN IRELAND** INTERNATIONAL WHO MADE MORE THAN 500 APPEARANCES FOR **ARSENAL**, WINNING THE DOUBLE, AND LATER MADE OVER 100 APPEARANCES FOR **WATFORD**.

6   HAVING WON THE FA CUP, THE LEAGUE AND THE UEFA CUP WINNERS' CUP WITH **EVERTON**, HE SPENT A SEASON AT **WATFORD** BEFORE JOINING **ARSENAL** IN 1987, WITH WHOM HE WON THE LEAGUE IN 1989. HE LATER WON THE 1994 LEAGUE CUP WITH **ASTON VILLA**.

7   **ENGLAND** STRIKER WHO WON HONOURS WITH **MANCHESTER UNITED** AND THE 2017 FA CUP WITH **ARSENAL**, BEFORE PLAYING FOR **WATFORD** AND **BRIGHTON & HOVE ALBION**.

"KENNY WHITE SHORTS"

NICKNAMED **"KENNY WHITE SHORTS"** FOR HIS ABILITY TO WIN THE BALL WITHOUT GOING TO GROUND, **KENNY SANSOM** WAS CAPPED 86 TIMES BY **ENGLAND** IN A CAREER THAT SAW HIM MAKE 768 CLUB APPEARANCES.

1 WITH WHICH CLUB DID HE LAUNCH HIS CAREER IN THE LATE 1970S, PROGRESSING FROM THE THIRD TIER TO THE OLD FIRST DIVISION?

2 WHO WAS THE MANAGER WHO SIGNED HIM TO **ARSENAL** IN 1980?

3 **KENNY SANSOM'S** TRANSFER TO **THE GUNNERS** INVOLVED AN EXCHANGE WITH WHICH STRIKER WHO HAD ONLY BEEN AT **ARSENAL** 62 DAYS AFTER SIGNING FROM **QUEENS PARK RANGERS?**

4 **SANSOM** CAPTAINED **ARSENAL** TO VICTORY OVER WHICH TEAM IN THE 1987 LEAGUE CUP FINAL?

5 **SANSOM** JOINED WHICH CLUB IN 1988, MANAGED AT THAT TIME BY **JIM SMITH?**

6 **TREVOR FRANCIS** SIGNED **SANSOM** TO WHICH CLUB IN 1989?

7 HE SPENT 1991 TO 1993 WITH **COVENTRY CITY** -- NAME ONE OF THE THREE MANAGERS HE PLAYED UNDER FOR THE **SKY BLUES**.

8 **HOWARD KENDALL** SIGNED **SANSOM** TO WHICH CLUB IN 1993?

9 **SANSOM** PLAYED ONCE, IN SEPTEMBER 1994, FOR WHICH CLUB?

10 NAME ONE OF THE TWO MANGERS WHO SELECTED **SANSOM** FOR **ENGLAND** BETWEEN HIS 1979 DEBUT AND HIS FINAL GAME IN 1988.

KINGS OF EUROPE!

NOTTINGHAM FOREST'S PLAYER OF THE YEAR IN 1977,
THE FOLLOWING SEASON SAW **TONY WOODCOCK** WIN A LEAGUE TITLE
AND A FOOTBALL LEAGUE CUP WITH HIS HOMETOWN CLUB, BE VOTED PFA
YOUNG PLAYER OF THE YEAR AND EARN THE FIRST OF HIS 42 **ENGLAND**
CAPS. THE NEXT SEASON BROUGHT THE EUROPEAN CUP AND A SECOND
LEAGUE CUP, BEFORE **WOODCOCK** SIGNED FOR **FC KÖLN**. FOLLOWING
THE 1982 WORLD CUP, HE JOINED **ARSENAL**, WHERE HE WAS THE CLUB'S
TOP SCORER FOR THREE SEASONS, BEFORE RETURNING TO GERMANY.

WITH WHICH CLUB DID THE FOLLOWING **ARSENAL** ALUMNI WIN A
EUROPEAN CUP OR UEFA CHAMPIONS LEAGUE?

1 GIOVANNI VAN BRONCKHORST

2 ALEX OXLADE-
CHAMBERLAIN

3 OLIVIER GIROUD

4 MARC OVERMARS

5 DAVOR ŠUKER

6 SERGE GNABRY

7 THOMAS VERMAELEN

8 MIKAËL SILVESTRE

9 SYLVINHO

10 NICOLAS ANELKA

11 ASHLEY COLE

12 JIMMY RIMMER

13 ALEXANDER HLEB

14 THIERRY HENRY

15 VIV ANDERSON

16 RAY KENNEDY

17 BRIAN KIDD

18 NWANKWO KANU

LEGENDARY LAWTON

HAVING MADE HIS LEAGUE DEBUT FOR **BURNLEY** AT THE AGE OF 16 YEARS AND 174 DAYS, **TOMMY LAWTON** JOINED **EVERTON** AT THE AGE OF 17 IN EARLY 1937. HIS 28 GOALS MADE HIM THE LEAGUE'S TOP SCORER IN 1937-38 AND THE FOLLOWING SEASON HE HELPED FIRE **THE TOFFEES** TO A LEAGUE TITLE, SCORING 35 GOALS IN 38 GAMES TO FINISH TOP LEAGUE SCORER ONCE MORE. LEAGUE FOOTBALL WAS SUSPENDED FOR THE DURATION OF THE SECOND WORLD WAR AND IN 1947, THIRD DIVISION **NOTTS COUNTY** BROKE THE BRITISH TRANSFER RECORD TO SIGN HIM FOR £20,000. AFTER HELPING THEM WIN PROMOTION, HE TOOK HIS SKILLS TO **BRENTFORD**, WHERE HE WAS ALSO PLAYER/ MANAGER FOR A WHILE, BEFORE ENDING HIS TOP FLIGHT PLAYING DAYS AT **ARSENAL**. DESPITE LOSING MANY OF HIS BEST YEARS TO THE WAR, **LAWTON** SCORED 260 GOALS IN 433 LEAGUE AND CUP COMPETITIONS IN 14 FULL SEASONS IN THE FOOTBALL LEAGUE. HE SCORED 22 GOALS FOR **ENGLAND** IN 23 APPEARANCES.

TOMMY LAWTON SCORED IN **ARSENAL'S** 3-1 WIN OVER **STANLEY MATTHEWS' BLACKPOOL** IN THE 1953 CHARITY SHIELD, THE COMPETITION NOW KNOWN AS THE COMMUNITY SHIELD.

THE TRADITIONAL SEASON OPENER PITS THE REIGNING CHAMPIONS AGAINST THE FA CUP WINNERS, ALTHOUGH THAT HAS VARIED ON OCCASION WHEN A CLUB HAS HAD PRIOR COMMITMENTS, OR WAS A LEAGUE AND FA CUP DOUBLE-WINNER, AND A REPLACEMENT TEAM HAS BEEN DRAFTED IN. **ARSENAL** HAVE WON 16 TIMES, INCLUDING 1991 WHEN THE TROPHY WAS SHARED WITH **TOTTENHAM HOTSPUR**.

IDENTIFY THESE OTHER CHARITY SHIELD/COMMUNITY SHIELD VICTORIES BY THE YEAR AND THE **ARSENAL** GOALSCORERS:

1 1930 : 2-1 -- SCORERS: **HULME, JACK**

2 1932: 1-0 -- SCORER: **BASTIN**

3 1933: 3-0 -- SCORERS: **BIRKETT (2), BOWDEN**

4 1934: 4-0 -- SCORERS: **BIRKETT, MARSHALL, DRAKE, BASTIN**

5 1938: 2-1 -- SCORERS: **DRAKE (2)**

6 1948: 4-3 -- **LEWIS(2), JONES, ROOKE**

7 1998: 3-0 -- SCORERS: **OVERMARS, WREH, ANELKA**

8 1999: 2-1 -- SCORERS: **KANU, PARLOUR**

9 2002: 1-0 -- SCORER: **GILBERTO**

10 2004: 3-1 -- SCORERS: **GILBERTO, REYES, SILVESTRE(O.G.)**

11 2014: 3-0 -- SCORERS: **CAZORLA, RAMSEY, GIROUD**

12 2015: 1-0 -- SCORER: **OXLADE-CHAMBERLAIN**

13 2017: 1-1 (WON ON PENALTIES) -- SCORER: **KOLAŠINAC**

14 2020: 1-1 (WON ON PENALTIES) -- SCORER: **AUBAMEYANG**

CAPTAINS FANTASTIC

NOT ONLY DID **TOM PARKER** CAPTAIN **ARSENAL** TO THE CLUB'S FIRST MAJOR TROPHY -- WHEN **ARSENAL** BEAT **HUDDERSFIELD TOWN** 2-0 TO WIN THE 1930 FA CUP -- HE LED **THE GUNNERS** TO A FIRST LEAGUE TITLE THE FOLLOWING YEAR. THE 1930 FINAL WAS NOTABLE FOR THE MID-GAME APPEARANCE OVER WEMBLEY OF THE LARGEST AIRSHIP EVER BUILT TO THAT POINT, THE 776-FOOT-LONG **GRAF ZEPPELIN.**

NAME THE CAPTAINS WHO LED **ARSENAL** TO VICTORY IN THE FOLLOWING FA CUP FINALS:

1   1936: 1-0 V **SHEFFIELD UNITED**

2   1950: 2-0 V **LIVERPOOL**

3   1971: 2-1 V **LIVERPOOL**

4   1979: 3-2 V **MANCHESTER UNITED**

5   1993: 1-1 V **SHEFFIELD WEDNESDAY** AND 2-1 REPLAY

6   1998: 2-0 V **NEWCASTLE UNITED**

7   2002: 2-0 V **CHELSEA**

8   2003: 1-0 V **SOUTHAMPTON**

9   2005: 0-0 V **MANCHESTER UNITED** (WON ON PENALTIES)

10   2014: 3-2 V **HULL CITY**

11   2015: 4-0 V **ASTON VILLA**

12   2017: 2-1 V **CHELSEA**

13   2020: 2-1 V **CHELSEA**

CITY SLICKERS

HAVING JOINED **ARSENAL** FROM **MARSEILLE** IN THE SUMMER OF 2008, **SAMIR NASRI** BOUNCED BACK FROM A BROKEN LEG AND THE DISAPPOINTMENT OF BEING LEFT OUT OF **FRANCE'S** 2010 WORLD CUP SQUAD TO BE NAMED 2010 FRENCH PLAYER OF THE YEAR. FOLLOWING A PROTRACTED TRANSFER WRANGLE, HE SIGNED FOR **MANCHESTER CITY** IN THE SUMMER OF 2011.

IDENTIFY THESE OTHER **ARSENAL** PLAYERS WHO ENDED UP AT **CITY:**

1 TWO-TIMES CHAMPIONS LEAGUE WINNER WITH **BARCELONA**, A BRAZILIAN LEFT-BACK WHO WON THE COMMUNITY SHIELD WITH **ARSENAL** IN 1999.

2 A UEFA CUP WINNERS' CUP WINNER WITH **THE GUNNERS** IN 1994, SCOTTISH STRIKER WHOSE SUBSEQUENT TRAVELS INCLUDED TWO SPELLS WITH **LEICESTER** AND TWO WITH **MANCHESTER CITY**.

3 **ENGLAND'S** SECOND MOST-CAPPED GOALKEEPER.

4 SON OF A **FULHAM** GREAT, A FULL-BACK OF ANGLO-ITALIAN HERITAGE WHO PLAYED FOR **ARSENAL**, **CITY** AND **READING** IN THE 1960S, EVENTUALLY MOVING INTO MANAGEMENT WITH A NUMBER OF TEAMS IN IRELAND.

5 **TOGO'S** ALL-TIME TOP GOALSCORER.

6 CAPPED 65 TIMES BY **FRANCE**, HE WON CUP HONOURS WITH **AUXERRE**, **ARSENAL** AND **CITY** BEFORE JOINING SERIE A SIDE **BENEVENTO** IN 2017.

7 CAPPED 120 TIMES BY THE **IVORY COAST**.

8 **ARSENAL** GREAT WHO WENT ON TO PLAY FOR **LEEDS UNITED**, **CITY** AND **CHELSEA**, HE DIED IN 2001 AT THE AGE OF 33.

9 IRISH STRIKER FOR **ARSENAL**, **CITY** AND **SUNDERLAND**, HE LATER BECAME CHAIRMAN OF **THE BLACK CATS**.

10 FRENCH STAR WHO WON FOUR FA CUPS AND THREE LEAGUE TITLES WITH *ARSENAL*, PLAYED FOR THREE SERIE A GIANTS AND HELPED *CITY* WIN THE 2011 FA CUP BEFORE GOING INTO COACHING AND MANAGEMENT.

YOUNG GUNS GUNNERS!

17-YEAR-OLD **NICOLAS ANELKA** SIGNED FOR **ARSENAL** IN EARLY 1997. HIS FIRST FULL SEASON SAW **THE GUNNERS** WIN THE DOUBLE AND THE FOLLOWING SEASON HE WAS **ARSENAL'S** TOP GOALSCORER AND WAS VOTED PFA YOUNG PLAYER OF THE YEAR.

IDENTIFY THESE OTHER **ARSENAL** PFA YOUNG PLAYERS OF THE YEAR:

1 1978: **ENGLAND** STRIKER WHO WAS PLAYING FOR **NOTTINGHAM FOREST** AT THE TIME.

2 1987: **ENGLAND** CAPTAIN WHO SPENT HIS ENTIRE PLAYING CAREER WITH **ARSENAL**.

3 1989: **ENGLAND** MIDFIELDER WHO WON THE FOOTBALL LEAGUE CHAMPIONSHIP TWICE, THE FA CUP, THE FOOTBALL LEAGUE CUP, AND THE EUROPEAN CUP WINNERS' CUP WITH ARSENAL BEFORE JOINING **MIDDLESBROUGH**. HE LATER WON HONOURS WITH **ASTON VILLA** AND **PORTSMOUTH** AND EVENTUALLY MOVED INTO TV PUNDITRY.

4 2008: **ARSENAL** PRODIGY WHO WOULD GO ON WIN TWO EUROS AND A WORLD CUP WITH **SPAIN**, AND LEAGUE TITLES AND MORE WITH **BARCELONA** AND **CHELSEA**.

5 2011: **ENGLAND** MIDFIELDER WHOSE SUBSEQUENT CLUBS INCLUDE **BOLTON WANDERERS**, **WEST HAM UNITED** AND **BOURNEMOUTH**.

AN ALL-TIME HIGH!

DENNIS BERGKAMP SCORED 37 GOALS IN HIS 79 APPEARANCES FOR THE **NETHERLANDS.** IN 1998, HE SURPASSED **FAAS WILKES'S** RECORD TO BECOME HIS COUNTRY'S TOP SCORER OF ALL TIME, A RECORD LATER ECLIPSED BY **PATRICK KLUIVERT.**

IDENTIFY THESE **ARSENAL** PLAYERS WHO ARE -- OR HAVE BEEN -- THEIR COUNTRY'S ALL-TIME TOP GOALSCORER:

1   51 GOALS FOR **FRANCE**, 1997-2010

2   50 GOALS FOR **NETHERLANDS**, 2005-2017

3   * 46 GOALS FOR **CHILE**, 2006-STILL ACTIVE AS OF 2021

4   45 GOALS FOR **CROATIA**, 1990-2002

5   32 GOALS FOR **TOGO**, 2000-2019

6   * 30 GOALS FOR **ARMENIA**, 2007-STILL ACTIVE AS OF 2021

7   * 27 GOALS FOR **GABON**, 2009-STILL ACTIVE AS OF 2021

8   21 GOALS FOR **REPUBLIC OF IRELAND**, 1986-2002

9   20 GOALS FOR **REPUBLIC OF IRELAND**, 1976-1990

OLD BOYS AND "THE OLD LADY"

FOLLOWING HIS IMPRESSIVE FORM FOR *ENGLAND* AT THE 1990 WORLD CUP, *ASTON VILLA'S DAVID PLATT* JOINED *BARI* IN THE SUMMER OF 1991. HIS FIRST SEASON IN ITALY ENDED IN RELEGATION FROM SERIE A, BUT HE WAS SNAPPED UP BY *JUVENTUS*. HE WON A UEFA CUP MEDAL WITH THE TURIN TEAM BEFORE JOINING *SAMPDORIA* IN 1993, WITH WHOM HE WON THE COPPA ITALIA, BEFORE SIGNING FOR *ARSENAL* IN 1995.

IDENTIFY THESE *ARSENAL* ALUMNI WHO HAVE ALSO PLAYED FOR THE CLUB THEY CALL *"LA VECCHIA SIGNORA"* -- "THE OLD LADY".

1 SIGNED FROM *JUVENTUS* IN 1999, HE WON THE PREMIER LEAGUE GOLDEN BOOT FOUR TIMES WITH *THE GUNNERS*.

2 WORLD CUP AND EUROS WINNER, HE WON HONOURS WITH *ARSENAL*, PLAYED A SEASON WITH *JUVENTUS* AND THEN WON HONOURS WITH *INTERNAZIONALE* AND *MANCHESTER CITY*.

3 *SENEGAL* INTERNATIONAL LOANED OUT BY *ARSENAL* TO *JUVENTUS* AND *PORTSMOUTH*, HIS SUBSEQUENT CLUBS INCLUDE *QUEENS PARK RANGERS*, *NOTTINGHAM FOREST* AND *CARDIFF CITY*.

4 DANISH STRIKER LOANED OUT BY *ARSENAL* TO *BIRMINGHAM CITY*, *SUNDERLAND* AND *JUVENTUS* BEFORE JOINING *VFL WOLFSBURG* IN 2014.

5 LEFT *ARSENAL* FOR *JUVENTUS* IN 2019 AND WON A SERIE A TITLE IN HIS DEBUT SEASON.

6 CAPPED 108 TIMES BY *SWITZERLAND*, RIGHT-BACK WHO WON A SERIE A TITLE IN EACH OF HIS SEVEN SEASONS WITH *JUVENTUS* BEFORE JOINING *ARSENAL* ON A FREE TRANSFER IN 2018.

7 *POLAND* GOALKEEPER WHO WON TWO FA CUPS AND THE PREMIER LEAGUE GOLDEN GLOVE WITH *ARSENAL* AND SPENT TWO SEASONS ON LOAN AT *ROMA* BEFORE JOINING *JUVENTUS* IN 2017.

8 *REPUBLIC OF IRELAND* GREAT WHO WON THE 1979 FA CUP WITH *THE GUNNERS* BEFORE WINNING TWO LEAGUE TITLES WITH *JUVENTUS*. HE LATER MANAGED *CELTIC*.

THE CENTURIONS

THE FIRST PLAYER TO APPEAR IN FIVE FA CUP FINALS WAS *ENGLAND* WINGER *JOE HULME.* HE WON IN TWO OF THE FOUR FINALS HE PLAYED IN AS AN *ARSENAL* PLAYER -- WITH WHOM HE ALSO GAINED THREE LEAGUE CHAMPIONSHIP MEDALS -- BEFORE PLAYING FOR *HUDDERSFIELD TOWN* ON THE LOSING SIDE IN THE 1938 FINAL.

HULME SCORED 125 GOALS FOR **ARSENAL** BEFORE SIGNING FOR
HUDDERSFIELD TOWN. THE PLAYERS LISTED BELOW ALSO RACKED UP A
CENTURY OR MORE OF GOALS FOR **THE GUNNERS** BEFORE SIGNING FOR
THEIR NEXT CLUB. NAME THE CLUB IN EACH CASE OR IF THEY RETIRED:

1   *THIERRY HENRY:* 228 GOALS

2   *IAN WRIGHT:* 185 GOALS

3   *CLIFF BASTIN:* 178 GOALS

4   *JOHN RADFORD:* 149 GOALS

5   *JIMMY BRAIN:* 139 GOALS

6   *TED DRAKE:* 139 GOALS

7   *DOUG LISHMAN:* 137 GOALS

8   *ROBIN VAN PERSIE:* 132 GOALS

9   *DAVID JACK:* 124 GOALS

10   *DENNIS BERGKAMP:* 120 GOALS

11   *REG LEWIS:* 118 GOALS

12   *ALAN SMITH:* 115 GOALS

13   *JACK LAMBERT:* 109 GOALS

14   *FRANK STAPLETON:* 108 GOALS

15   *THEO WALCOTT:* 108 GOALS

16   *DAVID HERD:* 107 GOALS

17   *OLIVIER GIROUD:* 105 GOALS

18   *JOE BAKER:* 100 GOALS

GUNNERS AND POTTERS

SON OF **MANCHESTER CITY** GOALKEEPER **ROY DIXON**, **LEE DIXON** PLAYED IN THE LOWER ECHELONS OF THE FOOTBALL LEAGUE, WITH **BURNLEY**, **CHESTER CITY**, **BURY** AND **STOKE CITY** BEFORE JOINING **ARSENAL** IN 1988. IN HIS 15 SEASONS WITH **THE GUNNERS**, **DIXON** WON FOUR LEAGUE TITLES AND THREE FA CUPS -- INCLUDING TWO LEAGUE AND CUP DOUBLES -- AND THE EUROPEAN CUP WINNERS' CUP.

NAME THESE OTHER **GUNNERS** WHO ALSO PLAYED FOR **STOKE CITY:**

1 HAVING WON TWO LEAGUE TITLES AND THE FA CUP IN HIS NINE SEASONS WITH **WOLVES** -- DURING WHICH TIME HE PLAYED FOR **ENGLAND** AT THE 1958 WORLD CUP -- A RIGHT-HALF WHO HAD A SEASON WITH **ARSENAL** BEFORE JOINING **STOKE CITY** IN 1962.

2 CENTRE-BACK WHO FOLLOWED SEVEN SEASONS WITH **THE POTTERS** WITH 11 SEASONS AT **ARSENAL**, DURING WHICH TIME HE WON THREE LEAGUE TITLES, TWO FA CUPS, THE LEAGUE CUP AND THE EUROPEAN CUP WINNERS' CUP. HE LATER SPENT 20 YEARS ON THE COACHING STAFF WITH **THE GUNNERS**.

3 FLAMBOYANT MIDFIELDER WHO WON THE 1971 EUROPEAN CUP WINNERS' CUP WITH **CHELSEA**, SPENT FOUR SEASONS AT **STOKE** AND PLAYED IN THE 1978 FA CUP FINAL WITH **ARSENAL**, BEFORE TAKING HIS SKILLS TO THE **SEATTLE SOUNDERS**. HE ENDED HIS CAREER BACK AT **STOKE** IN THE EARLY 1980S.

4 A MEMBER OF **ENGLAND'S** 1966 WORLD CUP-WINNING SQUAD, HIS CLUBS INCLUDED **NEWCASTLE UNITED**, **ARSENAL** AND **STOKE**. HE IS ALSO RENOWNED FOR A LANDMARK 1963 HIGH COURT CASE THAT IMPROVED FREEDOM OF MOVEMENT FOR PLAYERS.

5 WINGER WHO PLAYED MORE THAN 600 GAMES IN HIS TWO SPELLS WITH **COLCHESTER UNITED**, RACKED UP MORE THAN 100 APPEARANCES FOR **ARSENAL** IN THE MID-1980S AND HAD BRIEF SPELLS WITH **STOKE CITY** AND **LUTON TOWN**.

6 MUCH-TRAVELLED STRIKER ALSO KNOWN FOR HIS RESTAURANT BUSINESSES AND MARRIAGE TO TV STAR **LESLIE ASH**.

7 **SCOTLAND** STRIKER WHO LAUNCHED HIS CAREER WITH **STOCKPORT COUNTY**, WAS **ARSENAL** TOP SCORER IN FOUR OF HIS SEVEN SEASONS WITH **THE GUNNERS**, WON MAJOR HONOURS WITH **MANCHESTER UNITED** AND LATER PLAYED FOR **STOKE CITY** AND **WATERFORD**.

8 **ENGLAND** CENTRAL DEFENDER WHOSE CLUBS INCLUDED **LUTON TOWN, ARSENAL, BIRMINGHAM CITY, STOKE CITY, WEST HAM, BRIGHTON AND HOVE ALBION, LEICESTER CITY** AND **MK DONS** BEFORE RETIRING IN 2016.

TON-UP BOYS

BORN IN POLAND BUT RAISED IN GERMANY, **LUKAS PODOLSKI** ORIGINALLY FAVOURED PLAYING HIS INTERNATIONAL FOOTBALL FOR THE COUNTRY OF HIS BIRTH BUT WAS REJECTED BY **POLAND** COACH **PAWEL JANAS. LUKAS** WENT ON TO PLAY 130 TIMES FOR **GERMANY**, WINNING THE WORLD CUP AND BECOMING THE THIRD-HIGHEST GOALSCORER IN THE NATIONAL TEAM'S HISTORY.

NAME THESE **ARSENAL** PLAYERS WHO HAVE MADE A CENTURY OF APPEARANCES AT INTERNATIONAL LEVEL:

1 **CHILE:** 139 CAPS BETWEEN 2006 AND 2021 (STILL ACTIVE) *

2 **SWEDEN:** 133 CAPS BETWEEN 2008 AND 2021 (STILL ACTIVE) *

3 **SWEDEN:** 131 CAPS BETWEEN 2001 AND 2016

4 **CZECH REPUBLIC:** 124 CAPS BETWEEN 2002 AND 2016

5 **FRANCE:** 123 CAPS BETWEEN 1997 AND 2010

6 **ESTONIA:** 120 CAPS BETWEEN 1992 AND 2009

7 **IVORY COAST:** 120 CAPS BETWEEN 2000 AND 2015

8 **NORTHERN IRELAND:** 119 CAPS BETWEEN 1964 AND 1986

9 **SPAIN:** 110 CAPS BETWEEN 2006 AND 2016

10 **FRANCE:** 110 CAPS BETWEEN 2011 AND 2021 (STILL ACTIVE)*

11 **SWITZERLAND:** 108 CAPS BETWEEN 2006 AND 2019

12 **ENGLAND:** 107 CAPS BETWEEN 2001 AND 2014

13 **FRANCE:** 107 CAPS BETWEEN 1997 AND 2009

14 **NETHERLANDS:** 106 CAPS BETWEEN 1996 AND 2010

15 **CZECH REPUBLIC:**
105 CAPS BETWEEN 2000 AND 2016

16 **GERMANY:**
104 CAPS BETWEEN 2004 AND 2014

17 **COSTA RICA:**
103 CAPS BETWEEN 2011 AND 2021
(STILL ACTIVE)*

18 **NETHERLANDS:**
102 CAPS BETWEEN 2005 AND 2017

19 **ISRAEL:**
101 CAPS BETWEEN 1998 AND 2017

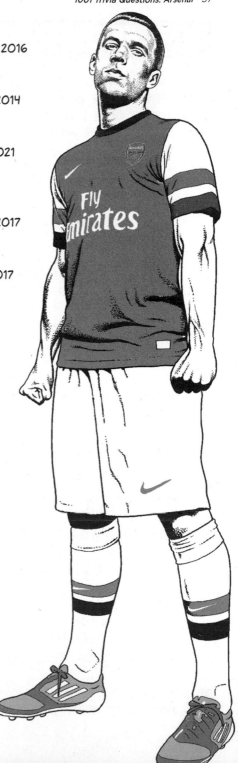

THE WRIGHT STUFF

ALTHOUGH *IAN WRIGHT* HAD TRIALS WITH *SOUTHEND UNITED* AND *BRIGHTON & HOVE ALBION* DURING HIS TEENS, HE WAS UNABLE TO WIN A PROFESSIONAL CONTRACT. WORKING AS A PLASTERER WHILE PLAYING FOR AMATEUR AND NON-LEAGUE TEAMS, IT SEEMED A CAREER IN FOOTBALL HAD PASSED HIM BY ... UNTIL WEEKS BEFORE HIS 22ND BIRTHDAY, HE WAS SIGNED TO *CRYSTAL PALACE* BY *STEVE COPPELL*.

1 IN 1985, HAVING PLAYED FOR BERMONDSEY SUNDAY LEAGUE SIDE *TEN-EM-BEE*, *WRIGHT* SIGNED FOR WHICH SEMI-PRO TEAM?

2 HE WAS SPOTTED AND SIGNED TO *CRYSTAL PALACE*, WHERE HIS PROLIFIC STRIKING PARTNERSHIP WITH WHICH FORMER *LEICESTER CITY* PLAYER HELPED FIRE *THE EAGLES* TO THE TOP FLIGHT?

3 HE SCORED TWICE AS A *"SUPERSUB"* IN THE 1990 FA CUP FINAL TO EARN A 3-3 DRAW AGAINST WHICH TEAM ? *(PALACE LOST THE REPLAY 1-0).*

4 WHO WAS THE MANAGER WHO GAVE *IAN WRIGHT* HIS FULL *ENGLAND* DEBUT IN 1991?

5 WHO WAS THE MANAGER WHO SIGNED HIM TO *ARSENAL* IN 1991?

6 HAVING SCORED ON HIS *ARSENAL* DEBUT, AGAINST *LEICESTER CITY* IN THE LEAGUE CUP, HE SCORED A HAT-TRICK AGAINST WHICH TEAM ON HIS LEAGUE DEBUT? *(HE SCORED ANOTHER HAT-TRICK AGAINST THE SAME TEAM ON THE FINAL DAY OF THE SEASON).*

7 DURING HIS SEVEN SEASONS WITH *THE GUNNERS*, HE WON THE FA CUP AND LEAGUE CUP IN 1993, THE EUROPEAN CUP WINNERS' CUP IN 1994 AND A LEAGUE AND FA CUP DOUBLE IN 1998. DURING THAT TIME HE SURPASSED WHICH PLAYER'S TALLY TO BECOME THE ALL-TIME TOP *ARSENAL* GOALSCORER, SETTING A RECORD THAT STOOD UNTIL 2005?

8 WHO WAS THE MANAGER WHO SIGNED *WRIGHT* TO *WEST HAM* IN 1998?

9 WHILE AT **WEST HAM**, HE WAS LOANED OUT TO WHICH CLUB?

10 WHO WAS THE MANAGER WHO SIGNED **WRIGHT** TO **CELTIC** IN 1999?

11 HE ENDED HIS PLAYING CAREER WITH A SPELL AT WHICH CLUB?

12 *IAN WRIGHT* WAS INDUCTED INTO THE ENGLISH FOOTBALL HALL OF FAME IN 2005, IN THE SAME YEAR AS WHICH **ARSENAL** AND **SCOTLAND** GREAT WHO WON FOUR LEAGUE TITLES AND TWO FA CUPS WITH **THE GUNNERS** IN THE 1930S?

GERMAN IMPORTS

A PRODUCT OF THE *AC MILAN* ACADEMY, *PIERRE-EMERICK AUBAMEYANG* WAS LOANED OUT TO A NUMBER OF CLUBS IN HIS NATIVE FRANCE, INCLUDING *DIJON*, *LILLE* AND *MONACO*, DURING WHICH TIME HE MADE HIS INTERNATIONAL DEBUT FOR *GABON*. A LOAN MOVE TO *SAINT-ÉTIENNE* WAS MADE PERMANENT IN 2011, *AUBAMEYANG* WINNING THE COUPE DE LA LIGUE BEFORE JOINING *BORUSSIA DORTMUND* IN 2013. IN FIVE SEASONS IN GERMANY HE GAINED CUP HONOURS AND WON BOTH BUNDESLIGA AND AFRICAN PLAYER OF THE YEAR AWARDS. HE SIGNED FOR *ARSENAL* IN EARLY 2018 IN A CLUB RECORD £56 MILLION DEAL.

FROM WHICH GERMAN CLUB DID *ARSENAL* SIGN:

1 *BERND LENO*

2 *PER MERTESACKER*

3 *GRANIT XHAKA*

4 *SOKRATIS PAPASTATHOPOULOS*

5 *TOMÁŠ ROSICKÝ*

6 *ALBERTO MÉNDEZ*

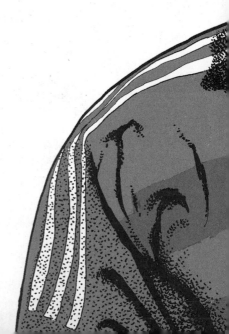

CZECH MARKS

IN 2000, 19-YEAR-OLD **TOMÁŠ ROSICKÝ** BECAME THE YOUNGEST-EVER PLAYER TO REPRESENT THE **CZECH REPUBLIC** IN A EUROPEAN CHAMPIONSHIP. WHEN HE APPEARED IN HIS FOURTH EUROS IN 2016, AT THE AGE OF 35, **"THE LITTLE MOZART"** BECAME THE OLDEST PLAYER TO REPRESENT HIS COUNTRY IN THE TOURNAMENT.

1 **ROSICKÝ** WAS NAMED CZECH FOOTBALLER OF THE YEAR THREE TIMES. WHICH **ARSENAL** TEAMMATE WON THE AWARD NINE TIMES?

2 **ROSICKÝ** BEGAN AND ENDED HIS CAREER WITH WHICH CZECH CLUB?

3 WHICH **CZECH REPUBLIC** FORWARD SPENT A BRIEF SPELL AT **ARSENAL** ON LOAN FROM **BANÍK OSTRAVA** IN 2003?

4 NAME THE SCOTTISH DEFENDER WHO MADE HIS DEBUT FOR **WOOLWICH ARSENAL** IN 1898 AND BECAME THE FIRST MAN TO PLAY 250 GAMES FOR THE CLUB, BEFORE LEAVING AFTER 14 YEARS TO COACH **SPARTA PRAGUE**, EVENTUALLY LEADING THEM TO A LEAGUE TITLE?

5 **ARSENAL'S** BIGGEST UEFA CHAMPIONS LEAGUE WIN CAME IN 2007 WITH A 7-0 THRASHING OF WHICH CZECH TEAM?

6 IN WHICH YEAR DID **THIERRY HENRY'S** TWO GOALS AGAINST **SPARTA PRAGUE** IN THE UEFA CHAMPIONS LEAGUE MAKE HIM THE ALL-TIME LEADING **ARSENAL** GOALSCORER?

7 WHEN **ARSENAL** PLAYERS TOOK A KNEE BEFORE THE 4-2 EUROPA LEAGUE WIN OVER **SLAVIA PRAGUE** IN 2021, THE GESTURE WAS A REACTION TO THE ABUSE OF WHICH FORMER **ARSENAL** PLAYER BY DEFENDER **ONDREJ KUDELA** IN A GAME BETWEEN **SLAVIA PRAGUE** AND **RANGERS?**

THE GUNNERS AND THE TRICKY TREES

RELEASED AS A SCHOOLBOY BY *MANCHESTER UNITED*, *VIV ANDERSON* BECAME AN INTEGRAL PART OF THE *NOTTINGHAM FOREST* TEAM THAT *BRIAN CLOUGH* CREATED, TAKING THE *"TRICKY TREES"* FROM THE SECOND DIVISION TO BECOME CHAMPIONS OF ENGLAND AND WIN TWO EUROPEAN CUPS. HE WON A LEAGUE CUP WITH *ARSENAL*, THE FA CUP IN HIS SECOND SPELL AT *UNITED* AND PLAYED FOR *SHEFFIELD WEDNESDAY*, *BARNSLEY* AND *MIDDLESBROUGH*.

IDENTIFY THESE *GUNNERS* WHO PLAYED FOR *NOTTINGHAM FOREST*:

1 MIDFIELDER WHO SPENT SEVEN YEARS WITH *ARSENAL*, SIX YEARS IN THE 1960S WITH *NOTTINGHAM FOREST* AND PLAYED BRIEFLY FOR *SHEFFIELD UNITED*, BEFORE EMBARKING ON A COACHING CAREER THAT SAW HIM MANAGE *PETERBOROUGH UNITED*, *WOLVES*, *AEK ATHENS*, *NOTTS COUNTY*, *WALSALL* AND *NORTHAMPTON TOWN* AND BECOME CHIEF EXECUTIVE OF THE LEAGUE MANAGERS ASSOCIATION.

2 STRIKER WHO WON LEAGUE, FA CUP AND EUROPEAN CUP WINNERS' CUP HONOURS WITH *ARSENAL* IN THE 1990S, EXPERIENCED RELEGATION AND PROMOTION WITH *FOREST*, AND LATER PLAYED FOR *TRABZONSPOR*, *EVERTON*, *WEST BROMWICH ALBION* AND *CARDIFF CITY*.

3 HAVING PLAYED IN ITALIAN FOOTBALL, *ENGLAND* STRIKER WHO WAS *ARSENAL'S* TOP SCORER IN THREE OF HIS FOUR SEASONS WITH *THE GUNNERS* BEFORE JOINING *FOREST* IN 1966. HE LATER PLAYED FOR *SUNDERLAND*, *HIBERNIAN* AND *RAITH ROVERS*.

4 LOANED TO *FOREST* AND *CARDIFF CITY* EARLY IN HIS *ARSENAL* CAREER, HE WON THREE FA CUPS WITH *THE GUNNERS* BEFORE HIS MOVE TO ITALY BROUGHT A SERIE A TITLE IN 2020.

5 SCOTTISH CENTRAL DEFENDER WHO PLAYED UNDER *TERRY NEILL* AT *SPURS* AND *ARSENAL*, JOINED *FOREST* IN 1981 AND LATER PLAYED FOR *NORWICH*, *BRIGHTON* AND *DARLINGTON*.

6 MIDFIELDER WITH *YORK CITY*, *NOTTINGHAM FOREST*, *ARSENAL* AND *SHEFFIELD UNITED*, HE LAUNCHED HIS MANAGEMENT CAREER AS A PLAYER AT *HEREFORD UNITED* AND WENT ON TO MANAGE CLUBS IN ENGLAND, WALES, SPAIN, SOUTH AFRICA, KUWAIT AND QATAR -- INCLUDING *DERBY COUNTY*, *ATLÉTICO MADRID* AND *SWANSEA CITY* -- BETWEEN 1971 AND 2004.

7 SIGNED TO *ARSENAL* FROM *CHARLTON ATHLETIC* IN 2011, RIGHT-BACK WHO SPENT THE LATTER HALF OF HIS FIVE SEASONS WITH *THE GUNNERS* ON LOAN AT *WEST HAM UNITED* AND *BIRMINGHAM CITY*, BEFORE SIGNING FOR *NOTTINGHAM FOREST* IN 2019.

8 CENTRE-FORWARD SIGNED FROM *LEYTON ORIENT* IN LATE 1958, HE WAS SENT OFF IN HIS FIRST FEW WEEKS WITH *THE GUNNERS* FOR KICKING *MAURICE NORMAN* OF *SPURS* IN A 4-1 WIN. HE SPENT THREE YEARS AT *FOREST* BEFORE BECOMING A *MILLWALL* LEGEND AFTER SCORING 35 GOALS IN A 59-GAME UNBEATEN RUN.

9 MIDFIELDER WHO, WHILE ON LOAN FROM *ARSENAL*, ACHIEVED CONSECUTIVE PROMOTIONS TO THE PREMIER LEAGUE WITH *NORWICH CITY* AND *WEST HAM UNITED*, BEFORE SIGNING FOR *FOREST* IN 2012. HE SPENT FOUR-AND-A-HALF-YEARS IN THE EAST MIDLANDS BEFORE JOINING *ASTON VILLA*. HE SIGNED FOR *LUTON TOWN* IN THE SUMMER OF 2021 AFTER A BRIEF SOJOURN AT *BRISTOL CITY*.

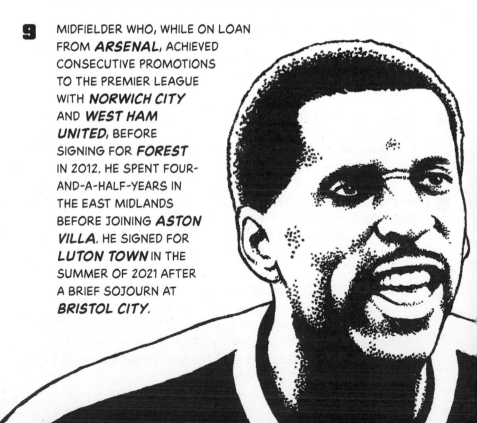

THE BOYS FROM BRAZIL

HAVING LAUNCHED HIS SENIOR CAREER IN HIS NATIVE BRAZIL WITH *VITÓRIA*, *DAVID LUIZ* WON LEAGUE AND LEAGUE CUP HONOURS WITH *BENFICA*, A PREMIER LEAGUE, TWO FA CUPS, THE UEFA CHAMPIONS LEAGUE AND TWO EUROPA LEAGUES WITH *CHELSEA*, TWO LEAGUE TITLES AND MULTIPLE CUP HONOURS WITH *PARIS SAINT-GERMAIN* AND THE FA CUP WITH *ARSENAL*. CAPPED 57 TIMES BY *BRAZIL*, HE REPRESENTED HIS COUNTRY AT THE 2014 WORLD CUP.

IDENTIFY THESE OTHER BRAZILIAN *GUNNERS:*

1 CENTRAL DEFENDER SIGNED FROM *LILLE* IN 2020 FOR AN ESTIMATED £27M AFTER ADD-ONS.

2 HAVING WON THE COPA LIBERTADORES AND FIFA CLUB WORLD CUP WITH *SÃO PAULO* IN 2005, MIDFIELDER WHO JOINED *ARSENAL* THE FOLLOWING YEAR. HE SPENT FIVE SEASONS WITH *THE GUNNERS*, PLAYING 153 TIMES, BEFORE RETURNING TO BRAZIL.

3 CENTRE-BACK SIGNED FROM *VILLARREAL* IN EARLY 2015, WON TWO FA CUPS WITH *ARSENAL* BEFORE JOINING *VALENCIA* IN 2017.

4 A DOUBLE WINNER IN 2002, HE ADDED A SECOND LEAGUE TITLE AND ANOTHER FA CUP TO HIS TALLY BEFORE LEAVING *THE GUNNERS* FOR *VALENCIA* IN 2005. HE WAS APPOINTED *ARSENAL'S* FIRST EVER TECHNICAL DIRECTOR IN 2019.

5 NICKNAMED *"THE BEAST"*, IN 2016 HE JOINED *ARSENAL* ON LOAN FROM *REAL MADRID* -- WITH WHOM HE HAD WON A LEAGUE TITLE -- IN AN EXCHANGE DEAL THAT SAW *JOSÉ ANTONIO REYES* MOVE IN THE OPPOSITE DIRECTION. HE WAS CAPPED 47 TIMES BY *BRAZIL*.

6 CAPPED 93 TIMES BY *BRAZIL*, HE WAS A MEMBER OF *"THE INVINCIBLES"*, THE TEAM THAT WENT UNDEFEATED THE WHOLE 2003-04 SEASON, AS WELL AS WINNING TWO FA CUPS. HE SCORED *ARSENAL'S* FIRST GOAL AT THE EMIRATES STADIUM, AS WELL AS SCORING IN JUST 21 SECONDS OF A UEFA CHAMPIONS LEAGUE GAME AGAINST *PSV EINDHOVEN* IN 2002.

7 SIGNED TO *ARSENAL* IN 2019, THE FIRST PLAYER TO SCORE FOUR TIMES IN HIS FIRST FOUR STARTS SINCE *IAN WRIGHT*, IN THE SUMMER OF 2021 HE WON AN OLYMPIC GOLD MEDAL WITH *BRAZIL*.

8 A COPA AMÉRICA WINNER WITH *BRAZIL* IN 2019, HE WON MULTIPLE HONOURS WITH *SHAKHTAR DONETSK* AND THEN *CHELSEA*, BEFORE MOVING ACROSS LONDON TO JOIN THE *GUNNERS* IN 2019.

THE BOYS OF 2005

ROBIN VAN PERSIE JOINED **ARSENAL** FROM **FEYENOORD** IN 2004. HE MADE HIS DEBUT IN THE 3-1 COMMUNITY SHIELD VICTORY OVER **MANCHESTER UNITED**, COMING ON AS A SUBSTITUTE. LATER IN HIS DEBUT SEASON, HE CAME ON AS A LATE SUBSTITUTE IN THE FA CUP FINAL AND SCORED ONE OF THE SHOOTOUT PENALTIES THAT GAVE **THE GUNNERS** ANOTHER VICTORY OVER **MANCHESTER UNITED**. ALTHOUGH **VAN PERSIE** SPENT ANOTHER SEVEN SEASONS WITH **ARSENAL** AND GAINED INDIVIDUAL AWARDS, THE 2005 FA CUP FINAL TROPHY WAS THE LAST PIECE OF SILVERWARE HE WON AS AN **ARSENAL** PLAYER. HE SIGNED FOR **MANCHESTER UNITED** IN THE SUMMER OF 2012 AND WON THE PREMIER LEAGUE IN HIS DEBUT SEASON.

WHICH CLUB DID THESE MEMBERS OF THAT 2005 FA CUP-WINNING TEAM JOIN WHEN THEY LEFT **ARSENAL?** (**DENNIS BERGKAMP**, WHO RETIRED AT THE END OF HIS **ARSENAL** CAREER, IS OMITTED FROM THE LIST).

1 JENS LEHMANN

2 LAUREN

3 KOLO TOURÉ

4 PHILIPPE SENDEROS

5 ASHLEY COLE

6 CESC FÀBREGAS

7 PATRICK VIEIRA

8 GILBERTO SILVA

9 ROBERT PIRES

10 MANUEL ALMUNIA

11 SOL CAMPBELL

12 *FREDDIE LJUNGBERG*

13 *EDU*

BETWEEN THE STICKS

AFTER JOINING **ARSENAL** IN THE SUMMER OF 2003, J**ENS LEHMANN'S** DEBUT SEASON SAW HIM PLAY IN EVERY MATCH OF THE SEASON AS **"THE INVINCIBLES"** WENT UNDEFEATED AND CLAIMED THE PREMIER LEAGUE TITLE. HAVING ADDED AN FA CUP TO HIS MEDAL TALLY, HE SPENT TWO SEASONS BACK IN GERMANY WITH **VFB STUTTGART** BEFORE COMING OUT OF RETIREMENT TO REJOIN **THE GUNNERS** DURING THE CLUB'S INJURY CRISIS IN EARLY 2011.

IDENTIFY THESE **ARSENAL** GOALKEEPERS

1 HAVING EARNED PROMOTION TO THE TOP FLIGHT WITH **LIVERPOOL** IN 1962, HE JOINED **ARSENAL** IN 1963, PLAYED IN THE 1968 LEAGUE CUP FINAL AND WENT ON TO PLAY FOR **ROTHERHAM UNITED** AND **PLYMOUTH ARGYLE.**

2 ITALIAN WHO SPENT MUCH OF HIS **ARSENAL** CAREER ON LOAN WITH **BARNSLEY** AND **HULL CITY**, WAS PLAYER OF THE YEAR AT **SUNDERLAND**, WAS NAMED MLS PLAYER OF THE YEAR WITH **MINNESOTA UNITED** WHILE ON LOAN FROM **READING**, AND SIGNED FOR **MONACO** IN 2020.

3 **MANCHESTER UNITED'S** BACK-UP GOALKEEPER IN THE 1968 EUROPEAN CUP-WINNING TEAM, HE WAS NAMED **ARSENAL** PLAYER OF THE YEAR DURING HIS THREE SEASONS WITH **THE GUNNERS** AND DURING HIS SIX SEASONS WITH **ASTON VILLA**, HE WON A LEAGUE TITLE AND BECAME ONLY THE SECOND MAN TO WIN A EUROPEAN CUP WINNERS' MEDAL AT TWO CLUBS.

4 GOALKEEPING GREAT WHO WON THE DOUBLE IN 1971 AND LATER SPENT 28 YEARS AS **ARSENAL'S** GOALKEEPING COACH WHILE CARVING OUT A CAREER AS A TV BROADCASTER.

5 A ONE-CLUB MAN WHO, BETWEEN 1949 AND 1963, PLAYED 352 GAMES FOR **THE GUNNERS** AND REPRESENTED **WALES** AT THE 1958 WORLD CUP.

6 **COLOMBIA** INTERNATIONAL SIGNED FROM **NICE** IN 2014, HE WON TWO FA CUPS WITH **ARSENAL** BEFORE JOINING **NAPOLI.**

7 **AUSTRIA** INTERNATIONAL WHO WAS **DAVID SEAMAN'S** UNDERSTUDY AT **ARSENAL** AND WHOSE CLUBS INCLUDE **FIORENTINA**, **JUVENTUS** AND **LIVERPOOL.**

8 A LEAGUE AND FA CUP DOUBLE WINNER IN HIS ONLY SEASON WITH **ARSENAL**, HIS CLUBS INCLUDED **EVERTON**, **SHEFFIELD UNITED** AND **MANCHESTER CITY** AND THREE SPELLS AT **IPSWICH TOWN.**

9 **POLAND** INTERNATIONAL WHOSE HONOURS INCLUDE TWO FA CUPS WITH **ARSENAL** AND THREE SERIE A TITLES WITH **JUVENTUS.**

GOING FULL THROSTLE!

ALTHOUGH HE SIGNED FOR **ARSENAL** IN 2005, WORK PERMIT RESTRICTIONS MEANT THAT **CARLOS VELA** DIDN'T ACTUALLY MAKE HIS DEBUT FOR **THE GUNNERS** UNTIL THREE YEARS LATER. DESPITE SCORING A HAT-TRICK ON HIS FIRST FULL START, HE SUBSEQUENTLY FAILED TO FORCE HIS WAY INTO **ARSÈNE WENGER'S** RECKONING. FOLLOWING A LOAN SPELL WITH **WEST BROMWICH ALBION**, HIS LOAN TO **REAL SOCIEDAD** WAS MADE PERMANENT IN 2012. AFTER SEVEN SEASONS IN SPAIN, HE SIGNED FOR **LOS ANGELES FC** IN 2018.

NAME THESE OTHER **GUNNERS** WHO HAVE PLAYED FOR **THE BAGGIES:**

1 LEFT-BACK WHO, HAVING WON THREE FA CUPS AND EARNED TEN **ENGLAND** CAPS IN HIS DOZEN SEASONS WITH **ARSENAL**, SIGNED FOR **WEST BROM** IN 2018. HE HELPED **THE BAGGIES** WIN PROMOTION IN 2020, BEFORE SIGNING FOR **INTER MIAMI** IN 2021.

2 A FIFA U-20 WORLD CUP WINNER WITH **ENGLAND** IN 2017, HE MADE HIS FULL INTERNATIONAL DEBUT IN 2020. A VERSATILE PLAYER WHO SPENT A SEASON ON LOAN WITH **IPSWICH** EARLY IN HIS CAREER AND WAS LOANED OUT BY **ARSENAL** TO **WEST BROM** IN 2021.

3 AN **ENGLAND** INTERNATIONAL FULL-BACK WHO SPENT A DOZEN YEARS WITH **WEST BROM**, DURING WHICH TIME HE WON THE FA CUP IN 1954, BEFORE ENDING HIS PLAYING DAYS WITH A COUPLE OF SEASONS AT **ARSENAL**. HE LATER MANAGED BOTH **WEST BROM** AND **ARSENAL**, AS WELL AS **GALATASARAY**, **QUEENS PARK RANGERS** AND **COVENTRY CITY**.

4 GERMAN WINGER WHO STARTED HIS CAREER AT **ARSENAL**, WHERE HE WAS LOANED OUT TO **WEST BROM** TO GAIN EXPERIENCE, BEFORE JOINING **WERDER BREMEN** IN 2016. HE JOINED **BAYERN MUNICH** THE FOLLOWING YEAR, WHERE HIS MEDAL HAUL TO DATE INCLUDES THREE LEAGUE TITLES (INCLUDING TWO LEAGUE AND CUP DOUBLES) AND THE UEFA CHAMPIONS LEAGUE.

5 **JAPAN** INTERNATIONAL WHOSE CLUBS INCLUDED **ARSENAL**, **FULHAM**, **WEST BROM**, **CARDIFF CITY**, **GALATASARAY**, **EINTRACHT FRANKFURT**, **STADE RENNES** AND MORE.

6 GOALKEEPER WHO WON FA CUP AND LEAGUE CUP MEDALS IN 1993 AND A EUROPEAN CUP WINNERS' CUP MEDAL IN 1994 -- ALL AS AN UNUSED SUBSTITUTE -- BEFORE HIS CAREER TOOK HIM TO A NUMBER OF CLUBS, INCLUDING *MIDDLESBROUGH, WEST BROM* AND *BLACKBURN ROVERS.*

7 DISENCHANTED AFTER BEING DEEMED SURPLUS TO REQUIREMENTS AT *ARSENAL,* HE SPENT SOME TIME PLAYING INDOOR SOCCER IN THE STATES BEFORE RETURNING TO ENGLAND TO BECOME PLAYER OF THE YEAR AT *WEST BROM,* A LEAGUE TITLE WINNER WITH *LEEDS UNITED* AND A SECOND DIVISION WINNER WITH *BIRMINGHAM CITY.*

8 FA CUP WINNER WITH *IPSWICH TOWN* IN 1978 AND *ARSENAL* IN 1979, HE PLAYED FOR *WATFORD, STOKE CITY* AND *FULHAM,* AS WELL AS PLAYING FOR AND LATER MANAGING *WEST BROM.*

9 *NIGERIA* STAR WHOSE HONOURS INCLUDED THREE LEAGUE TITLES AND THE UEFA CHAMPIONS LEAGUE WITH *AJAX,* THE UEFA CUP WITH *INTERNAZIONALE,* AND TWO LEAGUE TITLES AND TWO FA CUPS WITH *ARSENAL,* BEFORE WINNING THE FA CUP WITH *PORTSMOUTH* AFTER PLAYING FOR A COUPLE OF SEASONS WITH *WEST BROMWICH ALBION.*

"MAKING PLANS FOR NIGEL ..."

IN 13 YEARS WITH **ARSENAL, ENGLAND** FULL-BACK **NIGEL WINTERBURN** MADE 584 APPEARANCES AND WON A MULTITUDE OF HONOURS, INCLUDING THREE LEAGUE TITLES, TWO FA CUPS, A LEAGUE CUP AND THE EUROPEAN CUP WINNERS' CUP.

1 NAME ONE OF **WINTERBURN'S** TWO CLUBS BEFORE HE JOINED **WIMBLEDON** IN 1983.

2 WHO WAS THE MANAGER WHO SIGNED **NIGEL** TO **WIMBLEDON?**

3 **WINTERBURN** JOINED **ARSENAL** FOR £350,000 IN THE SUMMER OF 1987 -- WHO WAS THE MANAGER WHO SIGNED HIM?

4 HE EARNED JUST TWO **ENGLAND** CAPS, COMING ON AS A SUBSTITUTE AGAINST **ITALY** IN 1989 AND **GERMANY** IN 1993. WHO WERE THE TWO MANAGERS WHO SELECTED HIM?

5 **WINTERBURN** SCORED A SCREAMER AGAINST WHICH TEAM IN A 2-2 DRAW IN THE PENULTIMATE GAME OF THE 1988-89 SEASON, WHICH SET UP **ARSENAL'S** FABLED 2-0 WIN AT **LIVERPOOL** ON THE FINAL DAY OF THE SEASON TO CLINCH THE TITLE?

6 **WINTERBURN'S** CHALLENGE ON WHICH IRISH INTERNATIONAL SPARKED A 21-MAN BRAWL IN A GAME AGAINST **MANCHESTER UNITED** IN 1990, EARNING HIM A CLUB FINE AND A TWO-POINT DEDUCTION FOR **ARSENAL?**

7 **WINTERBURN** LEFT **ARSENAL** FOR WHICH CLUB IN 2000?

8 AFTER RETIRING IN 2003, HE WAS SUBSEQUENTLY APPOINTED AS DEFENSIVE COACH AT WHICH CLUB UNDER **PAUL INCE** IN 2008?

SIN BINNED!

MIDFIELDER **PAUL DAVIS** WON A MULTITUDE OF HONOURS WITH **THE GUNNERS**, INCLUDING TWO LEAGUE TITLES, THE FA CUP, TWO LEAGUE CUPS AND THE EUROPEAN CUP WINNERS' CUP. HE IS ALSO REMEMBERED FOR AN OFF-THE-BALL PUNCH THAT BROKE THE JAW OF **SOUTHAMPTON'S GLENN COCKERILL** AND EARNED HIM AN EIGHT-GAME BAN AND A £3,000 FINE IN 1988.

IDENTIFY THESE OTHER **ARSENAL** PLAYERS WHO EARNED BANS:

1 WHICH **SCOTLAND** INTERNATIONAL DEFENDER RECEIVED A SIX-WEEK BAN AND LOSS OF WAGES -- AT THE TIME, THE LONGEST BAN EVER GIVEN TO AN **ARSENAL** PLAYER -- FOR FIGHTING WITH **MANCHESTER UNITED'S DENIS LAW** IN A 1967 GAME?

2 NAME THE **FRANCE** INTERNATIONAL BANNED FOR SIX MATCHES AND FINED A RECORD £45,000 FOR SPITTING AT **WEST HAM UNITED'S NEIL RUDDOCK** AND AN ALTERCATION IN THE TUNNEL AFTER BEING SENT OFF IN 1999.

3 WHICH EX-**ARSENAL** STAR WAS BANNED FOR SIX MONTHS FOR FAILING A DRUGS TEST WHILE ON THE BOOKS OF **MANCHESTER CITY** IN 2011 -- WHICH HE BLAMED ON TAKING HIS WIFE'S DIET PILLS?

4 WHICH TWO DEFENDERS WERE BANNED FOR FOUR AND THREE MATCHES RESPECTIVELY -- AND FINED HEAVILY -- FOR THEIR PART IN A FRACAS AT THE END OF A 2003 GAME AGAINST **MANCHESTER UNITED** IN WHICH **RUUD VAN NISTELROOY** WAS JOSTLED?

5 WHICH **ARSENAL** DEFENDER WAS BANNED FOR FOUR MATCHES IN 2003 AFTER BEING SENT OFF FOR ELBOWING **MANCHESTER UNITED'S OLE GUNNAR SOLSKJÆR?**

6 WHICH DEFENDER WAS PILLORIED ON SOCIAL MEDIA IN LATE 2020 AFTER A RED CARD FOR GRABBING **BURNLEY'S ASHLEY WESTWOOD** BY THE THROAT EARNED HIM A THREE-GAME BAN?

7 BEFORE JOINING **ARSENAL** IN 1971, WHICH **ENGLAND** STAR RECEIVED A FIVE-WEEK BAN AND A £100 FINE AFTER RECEIVING THREE YELLOW CARDS PLAYING FOR **EVERTON** -- A SUSPENSION THAT REPORTEDLY COST HIM MORE THAN £1,000 IN WAGES AND BONUSES?

THEM'S THE BREAKS ...

IN 2008, MIDWAY THROUGH HIS DEBUT SEASON WITH **ARSENAL**, BRAZILIAN-BORN **CROATIA** INTERNATIONAL FORWARD **EDUARDO DA SILVA** SUFFERED A HORRIFIC INJURY IN A TACKLE THAT SAW **BIRMINGHAM CITY'S MARTIN TAYLOR** RED-CARDED. THE BROKEN LEFT FIBULA AND OPEN DISLOCATION OF HIS LEFT ANKLE SIDELINED **EDUARDO** FOR A YEAR AND DERAILED **ARSENAL'S** TITLE CHALLENGE.

IDENTIFY THESE OTHER INJURED **GUNNERS:**

1   WHEN GANGRENE SET IN AND ATE AWAY PART OF THE ANKLE TENDON, WHICH PLAYER'S 2016 ACHILLES INJURY REQUIRED EIGHT OPERATIONS AND SKIN GRAFTS AND WAS SO SEVERE THAT IT WAS THOUGHT AMPUTATION MIGHT BE REQUIRED?

2   IN 2007, WHICH **FRANCE** INTERNATIONAL'S DEBUT **ARSENAL** SEASON WAS ENDED BY AN ANKLE-BREAKING TACKLE FROM **SUNDERLAND'S DAN SMITH** THAT REQUIRED THREE SURGERIES AND EIGHT MONTHS' REHABILITATION?

3   SIGNED AS THE INTENDED REPLACEMENT FOR **DAVID SEAMAN** IN THE SUMMER OF 2002, WHICH **SWEDEN** GOALKEEPER BROKE HIS LEG IN TRAINING ON CHRISTMAS EVE, EFFECTIVELY ENDING HIS **ARSENAL** CAREER BEFORE IT HAD REALLY BEGUN?

4   WHICH **FRANCE** FULL-BACK SUFFERED A LEG BREAK TWICE IN THE SAME SEASON, RULING HIM OUT OF EURO 2012?

5   WHO SCORED THE WINNER IN THE 1993 LEAGUE CUP FINAL, ONLY TO BREAK HIS ARM IMMEDIATELY AFTER THE GAME WHEN **TONY ADAMS** TRIED TO PUT HIM ON HIS SHOULDERS BUT DROPPED HIM?

6   IN A 2010 UEFA CHAMPIONS LEAGUE GAME AGAINST **BARCELONA**, WHO SCORED A PENALTY WITH A BROKEN LEG?

7   WHICH INJURY-PLAGUED MIDFIELDER SUFFERED A FRACTURED ANKLE THAT RULED HIM OUT OF EURO 2012, A BROKEN FIBULA IN 2015 AND THEN A LEG FRACTURE IN 2017 ON LOAN WITH **BOURNEMOUTH?**

8   IN 2010, WHICH **ARSENAL** MIDFIELDER SUFFERED A DOUBLE LEG
FRACTURE IN A TACKLE BY **STOKE CITY'S RYAN SHAWCROSS?**

EAT OUR DUST!

THIERRY HENRY'S 30 LEAGUE GOALS IN THE 2003-04 SEASON WERE ENOUGH TO NOT ONLY WIN HIM THE PREMIER LEAGUE GOLDEN BOOT, THEY EARNED HIM THE EUROPEAN GOLDEN SHOE, THE AWARD GIVEN TO EUROPE'S TOP GOALSCORER EACH SEASON. THOSE GOALS HELPED FIRE **ARSENAL** TO THE CLUB'S 13TH TOP FLIGHT TITLE, OUTSTRIPPING NEAREST RIVALS **CHELSEA** BY 11 POINTS, THE LARGEST POINTS MARGIN IN THE CLUB'S TITLE-WINNING HISTORY.

NAME THE CLUBS WHO FINISHED SECOND TO **ARSENAL** IN THE FOLLOWING YEARS, OPPOSITION MANAGERS LISTED AS A CLUE:

1   1930-31: 7 POINTS - COMMITTEE SECRETARY **W.J. SMITH**

2   1932-33: 4 POINTS - COMMITTEE SECRETARY **W.J. SMITH**

3   1933-34: 3 POINTS - MANAGED BY **CLEM STEPHENSON**

4   1934-35: 4 POINTS - MANAGED BY **JOHNNY COCHRANE**

5   1937-38: 1 POINT - MANAGED BY **MAJOR FRANK BUCKLEY**

6   1947-48: 7 POINTS - MANAGED BY **MATT BUSBY**

7   1952-53: GOAL DIFFERENCE - MANAGED BY **SCOTT SYMON**

8   1970-71: 1 POINT - MANAGED BY **DON REVIE**

9   1988-89: GOALS SCORED - MANAGED BY **KENNY DALGLISH**

10   1990-91: 7 POINTS - MANAGED BY **GRAEME SOUNESS**

11   1997-98: 1 POINT - MANAGED BY **ALEX FERGUSON**

12   2001-02: 7 POINTS - MANAGED BY **GÉRARD HOULLIER**

"WHO IS MESSI? WHO IS NEYMAR?"

AS A YOUNGSTER, **JOEL CAMPBELL** WOULD JUGGLE EMPTY CANS ON THE STREETS OF SAN JOSE, COSTA RICA, WHERE HE WAS SPOTTED BY **COSTA RICA** MANAGER **RICARDO LA VOLPE**, WHO LATER CALLED HIM UP TO THE NATIONAL TEAM. **"WHO IS MESSI? WHO IS NEYMAR?"** SAID **LA VOLPE**, **"GENTLEMEN OF THE PRESS! I PRESENT TO YOU: CAMPBELL. I DISCOVERED HIM PLAYING WITH CANS"**. HE WAS STILL IN HIS TEENS WHEN HE SIGNED FOR **ARSENAL** IN 2011 BUT, UNABLE TO OBTAIN A WORK PERMIT, HE WAS LOANED OUT TO CLUBS IN FRANCE, SPAIN AND GREECE.

HE STARRED FOR **COSTA RICA** AT THE 2014 WORLD CUP, SCORING THEIR OPENING GOAL IN A 3-1 GROUP GAME WIN OVER **URUGUAY**. THE TEAM REACHED THE QUARTER-FINALS, WHERE IT REQUIRED A PENALTY SHOOTOUT FOR THE **NETHERLANDS** TO ADVANCE.

WHICH **ARSENAL** PLAYER -- PAST, PRESENT OR FUTURE -- SCORED THESE WORLD CUP GOALS:

1   1982: FOR **ENGLAND** V **FRANCE**, 3-1 WIN, GROUP STAGE

2   1990: FOR **REPUBLIC OF IRELAND** V **NETHERLANDS**, 1-1 DRAW, GROUP STAGE

3   1990: FOR **ENGLAND** V **BELGIUM**, 1-0 WIN, ROUND OF 16

4   1994: FOR **NETHERLANDS** V **BRAZIL**, 2-3 LOSS, QUARTER-FINALS

5   1998: FOR **FRANCE** V **BRAZIL**, 3-0 WIN, FINAL

6   1998: FOR **CROATIA** V **FRANCE**, 1-2 LOSS, SEMI-FINALS

7   2002: FOR **ENGLAND** V **SWEDEN**, 1-1 DRAW, GROUP STAGE

8   2006: FOR **FRANCE** V **BRAZIL**, 1-0 WIN, QUARTER-FINALS

9   2006: FOR **SWITZERLAND** V **SOUTH KOREA** 2-0 WIN, GROUP STAGE

10 2010: FOR *ENGLAND* V *GERMANY*, 1-4 LOSS, ROUND OF 16

11 2010: FOR *DENMARK* V *CAMEROON*, 2-1 WIN, GROUP STAGE

12 2010: FOR *NETHERLANDS* V *URUGUAY*, 3-2 WIN, SEMI-FINALS

13 2010: FOR *GERMANY* V *GHANA*, 1-0 WIN, GROUP STAGE

14 2014: FOR *FRANCE* V *SWITZERLAND*, 5-2 WIN, GROUP STAGE

15 2014: FOR *IVORY COAST* V *JAPAN*, 2-1 WIN, GROUP STAGE

16 2018: FOR *SWITZERLAND* V *SERBIA*, 2-1 WIN, GROUP STAGE

GUNNERS GONE GUVNORS

A TITLE WINNER WITH *EVERTON* IN 1939, *JOE MERCER* JOINED *ARSENAL* IN 1946, INSPIRING *THE GUNNERS* TO TWO LEAGUE TITLES AND AN FA CUP FINAL WIN. AS A MANAGER, AFTER ENJOYING SUCCESS WITH *ASTON VILLA*, HE LED *MANCHESTER CITY* TO UNPRECEDENTED GLORY, TAKING THEM FROM THE SECOND TIER TO LEAGUE, FA CUP, LEAGUE CUP AND EUROPEAN CUP WINNERS' CUP TRIUMPHS. HE ALSO HAD A SPELL AS CARETAKER MANAGER OF *ENGLAND*, RACKING UP THREE WINS AND THREE DRAWS IN HIS SEVEN GAMES IN CHARGE.

IDENTIFY THESE OTHER *GUNNERS* WHO WENT INTO MANAGEMENT:

1 CAPPED 107 TIMES BY THE *NETHERLANDS*, A MIDFIELDER WHO WON LEAGUE TITLES WITH *RANGERS*, *ARSENAL* AND *BARCELONA*. HE WON THE KNVB CUP WITH *FEYENOORD* AS BOTH A PLAYER AND THEN LATER AS MANAGER, BEFORE TAKING CHARGE OF *GUANGZHOU R&F* IN 2020.

2 A PREMIER LEAGUE WINNER WITH *ARSENAL* IN 1998, A *FRANCE* INTERNATIONAL WHO FREQUENTLY COVERED FOR *VIEIRA* AND *PETIT* IN MIDFIELD, HE WENT ON TO MANAGE FORMER CLUB *LYON*, *ASTON VILLA* AND *MONTREAL IMPACT*.

3 HE CAPTAINED *ARSENAL* TO THE INTER-CITIES FAIRS CUP AND THE 1971 DOUBLE BEFORE MANAGING HIS FORMER CLUB *LEICESTER CITY* AND SPENDING THREE YEARS AS *BRENTFORD* BOSS.

4 WELL-TRAVELLED PLAYER WHOSE CLUBS INCLUDED *COVENTRY CITY*, *ARSENAL*, *WEST BROM* AND TWO SPELLS AT *WOLVES*, HE MANAGED A NUMBER OF TEAMS INCLUDING *WIMBLEDON* -- WHO HE STEERED TO AN FA CUP FINAL WIN IN 1988 -- AND *WALES*.

5 WORLD CUP AND EUROS WINNER, WON HONOURS WITH *ARSENAL*, *INTERNAZIONALE* AND *MANCHESTER CITY* AND HAS MANAGED *NEW YORK CITY FC*, *NICE* AND *CRYSTAL PALACE*.

6 WORLD CUP WINNER WHO WON A LEAGUE TITLE WITH *EVERTON*, LOST AN FA CUP FINAL WITH *ARSENAL* AND MANAGED A STRING OF CLUBS, INCLUDING *STOKE CITY*, *MANCHESTER CITY*, *SOUTHAMPTON* AND TWO SPELLS IN CHARGE OF *PORTSMOUTH*.

7 *ARSENAL* LEGEND WHO MANAGED *MONACO* AND *MONTREAL IMPACT* AND HAS TWICE BEEN ASSISTANT *BELGIUM* MANAGER.

8 *ARSENAL* WING HALF, HE MANAGED *NORTHAMPTON TOWN* TWICE AND STEERED *WALES* TO THE 1958 WORLD CUP.

9 FA CUP WINNER WITH *IPSWICH* IN 1978 AND *ARSENAL* IN 1979, HE HAS MANGED IN ENGLAND, SCOTLAND AND CYPRUS.

10 *ARSENAL* ONE-CLUB LEGEND, CAPPED 66 TIMES BY *ENGLAND*, HE MANAGED *WYCOMBE WANDERERS*, *PORTSMOUTH*, AZERBAIJANI SIDE *GABALA* AND SPANISH SIDE *GRANADA*.

"SAFE HANDS" SEAMAN

CAPPED 75 TIMES BY **ENGLAND**, **DAVID SEAMAN** WON THREE LEAGUE TITLES, FOUR FA CUPS, THE LEAGUE CUP AND THE EUROPEAN CUP WINNERS' CUP DURING HIS 13 SEASONS WITH **THE GUNNERS**.

1 *SEAMAN* BEGAN HIS CAREER AT WHICH YORKSHIRE CLUB?

2 AGED 19, HE JOINED WHICH FOURTH DIVISION TEAM, WHERE HE WAS VOTED CLUB PLAYER OF THE YEAR IN HIS SECOND SEASON?

3 MANAGER *RON SAUNDERS* SIGNED HIM TO WHICH SECOND-TIER CLUB IN 1984, *SEAMAN* EXPERIENCING PROMOTION AND RELEGATION IN HIS TWO SEASONS THERE?

4 HE JOINED *QUEENS PARK RANGERS* IN AUGUST, 1986. NAME ONE OF THE THREE MANAGERS UNDER WHOM HE PLAYED BEFORE SIGNING FOR *ARSENAL* IN MAY, 1990.

5 NAME THE MANAGER WHO GAVE *SEAMAN* HIS *ENGLAND* DEBUT IN LATE 1988, WHILE THE GOALKEEPER WAS STILL A *QPR* PLAYER.

6 WHO WAS THE *ARSENAL* MANAGER WHO SIGNED *SEAMAN* FOR A BRITISH GOALKEEPER RECORD FEE OF £1.3 MILLION?

7 *SEAMAN'S* FINAL ACT AS AN *ARSENAL* PLAYER WAS TO LIFT THE FA CUP AS CAPTAIN IN 2003, HAVING KEPT A CLEAN SHEET IN A 1-0 WIN OVER WHICH OPPONENTS?

8 HE ENDED HIS CAREER WITH A BRIEF SPELL AT WHICH CLUB MANAGED BY *KEVIN KEEGAN?*

9 WHO WAS THE MANAGER WHO GAVE *SEAMAN* HIS FINAL *ENGLAND* CAP IN LATE 2002?

10 *SEAMAN* MARRIED *FRANKIE POULTNEY* IN 2015. THEY WERE PARTNERED ON THE FIRST AND NINTH SERIES OF WHICH TV SERIES?

NORN IRON BOYS

TERRY NEILL WAS ONLY 20 YEARS OLD WHEN HE WAS MADE THE YOUNGEST CAPTAIN IN **ARSENAL'S** HISTORY. A VERSATILE MIDFIELDER, HE ALSO CAPTAINED **NORTHERN IRELAND**, MAKING 59 APPEARANCES FOR HIS COUNTRY. HE PLAYED 275 TIMES FOR **ARSENAL** BEFORE JOINING **HULL CITY** AS PLAYER/MANAGER IN 1970. THE NEXT YEAR, HE ALSO TOOK ON THE SAME ROLE FOR **NORTHERN IRELAND** ON A PART-TIME BASIS. TWO YEARS MANAGING **TOTTENHAM HOTSPUR** WERE FOLLOWED BY HIS APPOINTMENT AS MANAGER OF **ARSENAL** IN 1976. HE STEERED THE CLUB TO THREE FA CUP FINALS, WINNING ONCE, AND THE 1980 FINAL OF THE UEFA CUP WINNERS' CUP. HIS REIGN AT **ARSENAL** ENDED IN 1983.

1 WHICH GOALKEEPER BROKE *TERRY NEILL'S* APPEARANCE RECORD FOR *NORTHERN IRELAND*, EVENTUALLY PLAYING 119 TIMES FOR HIS COUNTRY, A RECORD THAT STOOD UNTIL 2020?

2 NAME THE *ARSENAL* RIGHT-BACK WHO SPENT SIX SEASONS AT *HIGHBURY* AFTER SIGNING FROM *PORTADOWN* IN 1959, BEFORE SPENDING THREE SEASONS WITH *BRIGHTON & HOVE ALBION*. CAPPED 26 TIMES BY *NORTHERN IRELAND*, HE LATER COACHED AND MANAGED IN DANISH FOOTBALL.

3 NAME THE *ARSENAL* GOALKEEPER OF THE EARLY 1960S, A *NORTHERN IRELAND* INTERNATIONAL, WHO LATER PLAYED FOR *FULHAM*, *LINCOLN CITY* AND *BARNET* BEFORE TRAGICALLY SUCCUMBING TO A BRAIN TUMOUR AT THE AGE OF 35.

4 CAPPED 49 TIMES BY *NORTHERN IRELAND*, WHICH RIGHT-BACK MADE MORE THAN 500 APPEARANCES FOR *THE GUNNERS*, WINNING THE DOUBLE IN 1971 AND THE FA CUP IN 1979, BEFORE HELPING *WATFORD* GAIN PROMOTION TO THE TOP FLIGHT AND REACH AN FA CUP FINAL? HE LATER BECAME A MEMBER OF THE COACHING STAFF AT *ARSENAL* AND -- LIKE *BOB WILSON* -- HAS THE HONOUR OF FIGURING IN ALL THREE *ARSENAL* DOUBLE TRIUMPHS, AS A PLAYER AND COACH.

5 WHICH YOUNG *ARSENAL* DEFENDER, WHO HAS SPENT TIME ON LOAN AT *SWINDON TOWN*, *BLACKPOOL* AND *MILLWALL*, MADE HIS *NORTHERN IRELAND* DEBUT IN 2019?

6 CAPPED 51 TIMES BY *NORTHERN IRELAND*, FOR WHOM HE PLAYED AT THE 1982 WORLD CUP, WHICH LEFT-BACK SPENT 15 YEARS WITH *ARSENAL* -- WINNING THE FA CUP IN 1979 -- BEFORE ENDING HIS CAREER WITH TWO SEASONS AT *BRIGHTON & HOVE ALBION?*

7 CAPPED 39 TIMES BY *NORTHERN IRELAND*, WHOSE GOAL WON THE 1993 LEAGUE CUP FINAL FOR *ARSENAL?*

8 NICKNAMED *"FLINT"*, WHICH DEFENDER PLAYED MORE THAN 300 GAMES FOR *ARSENAL* BETWEEN 1958 AND 1966 -- DURING WHICH TIME HE WAS CAPPED 10 TIMES FOR *NORTHERN IRELAND* -- BEFORE JOINING *MILLWALL?*

VIVA ESPAÑA

BARCELONA-BORN *HÉCTOR BELLERÍN* PLAYED FOR *SPAIN* AT A NUMBER OF YOUTH LEVELS, REACHING THE SEMI-FINALS OF THE 2013 EUROPEAN CHAMPIONSHIP WITH THE UNDER-19 TEAM, BEFORE MAKING HIS SENIOR DEBUT IN 2016.

IDENTIFY THESE OTHER SPANISH *GUNNERS:*

1 SPAIN'S PLAYER OF THE YEAR IN 2007, HE WAS CAPPED 81 TIMES BY *SPAIN*, WITH WHOM HE WON EUROPEAN CHAMPIONSHIPS IN 2008 AND 2012, HAD THREE SPELLS WITH *VILLARREAL*, WON TWO FA CUPS WITH *ARSENAL* AND NUMEROUS HONOURS WITH *AL SADD*.

2 MIDFIELDER WHO SPENT PART OF 2019 ON LOAN AT *ARSENAL* FROM *BARCELONA*, AFTER WHICH HE SIGNED FOR CELTA. HIS PREVIOUS CLUBS WERE *MANCHESTER CITY* AND *SEVILLA*.

3 MIDFIELDER WHO WON A WORLD CUP AND TWO EUROPEAN CHAMPIONSHIPS AS HE RACKED UP MORE THAN A CENTURY OF *SPAIN* CAPS, HE HAS WON MULTIPLE HONOURS WITH *ARSENAL*, *BARCELONA*, *CHELSEA* AND *MONACO*.

4 SIGNED AS A BACKUP FOR *JENS LEHMANN*, HE MADE 175 APPEARANCES IN SEVEN SEASONS AT *ARSENAL*, LATER PLAYING FOR *WEST HAM UNITED* AND *WATFORD*.

5 SPANISH CENTRE-BACK WHO JOINED *ARSENAL* FROM BRAZIL'S *FLAMENGO* IN 2020, HIS PREVIOUS CLUBS INCLUDE *MALLORCA*, *MANCHESTER CITY*, *NAC BREDA* AND *DEPORTIVO DE LA CORUÑA*.

6 HIS CLUBS INCLUDED *BARCELONA*, *RANGERS*, *PSG*, *EVERTON* AND *ARSENAL* BEFORE GOING INTO COACHING AND MANAGEMENT.

7 *SPAIN* INTERNATIONAL SIGNED FROM *MÁLAGA* IN 2003, HE WON THREE FA CUPS WITH *ARSENAL* BEFORE JOINING *REAL SOCIEDAD* IN 2019.

MEET THE NEW BOSS, SAME AS THE OLD BOSS

HAVING JOINED **ARSÈNE WENGER'S MONACO** AS A TEEN, **EMMANUEL PETIT** WON THE COUPE DE FRANCE AND PLAYED IN THE 1992 EUROPEAN CUP WINNERS' CUP FINAL, WHICH **MONACO** LOST TO **WERDER BREMEN. WENGER** LEFT TO TAKE UP THE REINS AT **ARSENAL** IN 1994 AND **PETIT** FOLLOWED HIM THERE IN 1997, AFTER CAPTAINING **MONACO** TO A LEAGUE TITLE.

1 UNDER WHICH MANAGER DID **PAT JENNINGS** PLAY AT BOTH **TOTTENHAM HOTSPUR** AND **ARSENAL?**

2 WHICH **ENGLAND** FULL-BACK PLAYED UNDER **DON HOWE** AT **ARSENAL, QUEENS PARK RANGERS** AND **COVENTRY CITY?**

3 WHICH WORLD CUP WINNER PLAYED UNDER **WENGER** AT **MONACO** AND **ARSENAL**, EITHER SIDE OF A SPELL WITH **JUVENTUS?**

4 WHICH **SCOTLAND** CENTRE-HALF PLAYED UNDER **TERRY NEILL** AT **SPURS** AND **ARSENAL** BEFORE JOINING **NOTTINGHAM FOREST?**

5 **EDDIE MCGOLDRICK** LEFT **ARSENAL** FOR **MANCHESTER CITY** IN 1993 AND WAS REUNITED WITH HIS FORMER **CRYSTAL PALACE** BOSS -- ONLY FOR THAT MANAGER TO QUIT A MONTH INTO THE JOB! WHO WAS THAT MANAGER?

6 **PAUL MERSON** PLAYED UNDER **GRAHAM TAYLOR** FOR **ENGLAND** AND AT WHICH CLUB?

7 **PAUL MARINER** PLAYED UNDER **BOBBY ROBSON** FOR **ENGLAND** AND AT WHICH CLUB?

8 **STEWART ROBSON** PLAYED UNDER **DON HOWE** AT **ARSENAL** AND WHICH OTHER CLUB?

9 UNDER WHICH MANAGER DID *NIALL QUINN* PLAY AT *MANCHESTER CITY* AND *SUNDERLAND?*

10 UNDER WHICH MANAGER DID *CLIVE ALLEN* PLAY AT *CRYSTAL PALACE, QUEENS PARK RANGERS* AND *SPURS?*

HE'S A KEEPER!

31-YEAR-OLD SPANIARD **MANUEL ALMUNIA**, AN FA CUP WINNER
WITH **ARSENAL**, RETIRED IN 2014 ON MEDICAL ADVICE, AFTER A RARE
HEART CONDITION WAS PICKED UP DURING A MEDICAL WITH SERIE A SIDE
CAGLIARI CALCIO. NAME THE NATIONALITY OF THESE GOALKEEPERS:

1 **WOJCIECH SZCZĘSNY**

2 **BERND LENO**

3 **JACK KELSEY**

4 **ALEX MANNINGER**

5 **RAMI SHAABAN**

6 **MART POOM**

GONE TOO SOON

JOSÉ ANTONIO REYES MADE HIS DEBUT FOR *SEVILLA* AT THE AGE OF 16 AND HELPED THE CLUB SECURE PROMOTION TO THE TOP FLIGHT BEFORE JOINING *ARSENAL* IN EARLY 2004. HE WON THE PREMIER LEAGUE IN HIS DEBUT SEASON AND THE FA CUP IN HIS SECOND. ON LOAN AT *REAL MADRID* HE WON LA LIGA IN 2007, BEFORE JOINING *ATLÉTICO MADRID,* WITH WHOM HE WON TWO EUROPA LEAGUES AND THE UEFA SUPER CUP -- AND A PORTUGUESE LEAGUE CUP ON LOAN WITH *BENFICA!* A RETURN TO *SEVILLA* IN EARLY 2012 SAW HIM WIN THREE MORE EUROPA LEAGUE MEDALS. CAPPED 21 TIMES BY *SPAIN*, HE ENDED HIS CAREER WITH A BRIEF SPELL IN CHINA AND IN THE LOWER ECHELONS OF SPANISH FOOTBALL. HE WAS KILLED IN A 2019 CAR CRASH IN SPAIN, AT THE AGE OF 35.

1 HAVING WON TWO LEAGUE TITLES AND A LEAGUE CUP WITH *ARSENAL,* AND PLAYED FOR *LEEDS UNITED, MANCHESTER CITY, CHELSEA, NORWICH CITY* AND *HULL CITY,* WHICH *ENGLAND* INTERNATIONAL SUCCUMBED TO NON-HODGKIN'S LYMPHOMA IN 2001 AT THE AGE OF 33?

2 WHICH GOALKEEPER WON LEAGUE CUP, FA CUP AND EUROPEAN CUP WINNERS' CUP MEDALS IN THE 1990S WITH *ARSENAL* -- AS AN UNUSED SUBSTITUTE -- BEFORE A CAREER THAT SAW HIM WIN PROMOTION WITH *MIDDLESBROUGH* AND A LEAGUE CUP WITH *BLACKBURN ROVERS,* AND PASSED AWAY IN 2021 AGED 51?

3 WHICH ITALIAN TEENAGER, AN FA YOUTH CUP WINNER WITH *ARSENAL* IN 2000, WAS KILLED IN 2001 WHILE RIDING HIS MOPED HOME FROM A TRAINING SESSION WHILE ON LOAN AT *BOLOGNA?*

4 CAN YOU NAME THE *WOOLWICH ARSENAL* FULL-BACK WHO BROKE HIS ARM IN AN 1896 GAME AGAINST *KETTERING,* CONTRACTED BLOOD POISONING AND TETANUS, AND DESPITE HAVING THE ARM AMPUTATED, DIED SIX DAYS LATER AT THE AGE OF 26?

5 WHICH CENTRE-HALF, SIGNED FROM *MANCHESTER CITY* IN 1983, LATER CAPTAINED *OXFORD UNITED* AND PLAYED FOR *CHARLTON ATHLETIC,* DIED OF A HEART ATTACK AT THE AGE OF 30 IN 1993, A MONTH AFTER ANNOUNCING HIS RETIREMENT?

NERAZZURRI O ROSSONERI

DENNIS BERGKAMP'S DEBUT SEASON WITH **INTERNAZIONALE** SAW THE **"NERAZZURRI"** FLIRT WITH RELEGATION FROM SERIE A BUT WIN THE UEFA CUP. HAMPERED BY INJURY AND FATIGUE FOLLOWING THE 1994 WORLD CUP, **BERGKAMP'S** FORM SLUMPED SO BADLY IN HIS SECOND SEASON THAT ONE NEWSPAPER GAVE HIM A **"DONKEY OF THE WEEK"** AWARD. HE MOVED TO **ARSENAL** IN THE SUMMER OF 1995 ... AND OVER HIS ELEVEN SEASONS IN LONDON, ESTABLISHED HIMSELF AS ONE OF THE GREATEST PLAYERS IN THE HISTORY OF **THE GUNNERS**.

NAME THESE **GUNNERS** WHO PLAYED FOR ONE OF THE MILAN CLUBS:

1 POLISH-BORN WORLD CUP WINNER WITH **GERMANY** WHO JOINED **INTERNAZIONALE** ON LOAN FROM **ARSENAL** IN 2015.

2 FRENCH MIDFIELDER WHO WON AN FA CUP WITH **ARSENAL**, THE 2011 SERIE A TITLE WITH **AC MILAN**, RETURNED TO **ARSENAL** TO WIN TWO MORE FA CUPS AND THEN LATER PLAYED FOR **CRYSTAL PALACE** AND **GETAFE**.

3 **ARSENAL** LEGEND WHOSE THREE LEAGUE TITLES AND FOUR FA CUPS INCLUDE THE 1998 AND 2002 DOUBLES, HE PLAYED FOR **JUVENTUS** AND BOTH MILAN CLUBS -- WINNING THREE LEAGUE TITLES WITH **INTERNAZIONALE** -- AND ENDED HIS PLAYING DAYS AT **MANCHESTER CITY** WHERE HE WON ANOTHER FA CUP.

4 CAPPED 40 TIMES BY **FRANCE**, HE LEFT **INTERNAZIONALE** FOR **MANCHESTER UNITED** IN 1999, WHERE HE WON A PLETHORA OF HONOURS OVER NINE SEASONS, THEN SPENT TWO SEASONS AT **ARSENAL** BEFORE JOINING **WERDER BREMEN** IN 2010.

5 TWICE AN FA CUP WINNER WITH **ARSENAL** BEFORE JOINING **MANCHESTER UNITED**, A CHILEAN WHO HAS WON LEAGUE TITLES WITH **COLO-COLO**, **RIVER PLATE** AND **BARCELONA**.

6 CAPPED 39 TIMES BY **ARGENTINA**, FULL-BACK WHO PLAYED 69 TIMES FOR **ARSENAL** BEFORE JOINING **INTERNAZIONALE** IN 2001.

7 GRADUATE OF THE *AC MILAN* YOUTH ACADEMY WHO WON HONOURS WITH *SAINT-ÉTIENNE* AND *BORUSSIA DORTMUND* BEFORE JOINING *ARSENAL* IN EARLY 2018.

8 SWISS CENTRE-BACK LOANED OUT BY *ARSENAL* TO *AC MILAN* AND *EVERTON* BEFORE JOINING *FULHAM* IN 2010.

9 WORLD CUP-WINNING *FRANCE* STRIKER WHO PLAYED FOR *ARSENAL* AND *CHELSEA* BEFORE JOINING *AC MILAN* IN THE SUMMER OF 2021.

10 *NIGERIA* STRIKER WHO JOINED *ARSENAL* IN EARLY 1999 AFTER WINNING THE UEFA CUP WITH *INTERNAZIONALE*.

11 GERMAN GOALKEEPER WHO HAD PLAYED FOR *SCHALKE 04*, *AC MILAN* AND *BORUSSIA DORTMUND* BEFORE HIS FIRST SPELL WITH *ARSENAL* IN 2003.

12 *REPUBLIC OF IRELAND* AND *ARSENAL* GREAT WHO PLAYED FOR *JUVENTUS*, *SAMPDORIA*, *ASCOLI* AND *INTERNAZIONALE* IN THE 1980S.

"SHAKE MY LITTLE TUSHY ON THE CATWALK ..."

WINNER OF TWO PREMIER LEAGUES AND THREE FA CUPS WITH **ARSENAL,** **SWEDEN** INTERNATIONAL **FREDDIE LJUNGBERG** REPRESENTED HIS COUNTRY AT FIVE MAJOR TOURNAMENTS AND PLAYED WITH CLUBS IN SWEDEN, SCOTLAND, THE UNITED STATES, JAPAN AND INDIA. HIS GOOD LOOKS BROUGHT MODELLING ASSIGNMENTS FOR A NUMBER OF TOP BRANDS INCLUDING **PROCTER & GAMBLE,** **L'ORÉAL,** **BEATS,** **PEPSI** AND -- MOST FAMOUSLY -- **CALVIN KLEIN UNDERWEAR!**

1 WHICH ARSENAL PLAYER LAUNCHED HIS OWN **M10 STEETWEAR** BRAND OF CLOTHING IN LATE 2020?

2 WHICH **ARSENAL** GOALKEEPER ONCE DONNED A GIANT OIL FILTER COSTUME IN A TV COMMERCIAL FOR **UNIPART?**

3 WHICH **ARSENAL** STAR SIGNED A CONTRACT WITH THE PRESTIGIOUS **ELITE MODEL MANAGEMENT** AGENCY IN 2014?

4 WHICH MIDFIELDER, WHO BEGAN HIS CAREER AT **ARSENAL** AND PLAYED FOR CLUBS INCLUDING **STOKE CITY,** **READING,** **BRENTFORD** AND **ALDERSHOT TOWN,** BECAME A VERY SUCCESSFUL MODEL WITH CLIENTS INCLUDING **SCOTCH & SODA,** **THOMAS PINK,** **VINCE,** **GIORGIO ARMANI** AND **GQ MAGAZINE?**

5 WHICH **ARSENAL** AND **ENGLAND** STRIKER DONNED A VELVET JACKET AND CRAVAT TO PROMOTE **"SIZZLE & STIR"** SAUCES IN A TV COMMERCIAL FOR THE **CHICKEN TONIGHT** BRAND?

6 WHICH **ARSENAL** STAR TOOK TO THE CATWALK AT PARIS FASHION WEEK MODELLING BRIGHT PINK **LOUIS VUITTON** IN 2019 AND LAUNCHED HIS OWN CLOTHING LINE WITH **H&M** IN 2021?

7 WHICH **ARSENAL** GREAT WAS TEAMED WITH **ROGER FEDERER** AND **TIGER WOODS** TO ADVERTISE **GILLETTE** RAZORS?

8 WHICH **ARSENAL** PLAYER WAS SHOWN CLUTCHING A BLOODY COW'S HEART IN A CONTROVERSIAL 2014 WORLD CUP **ADIDAS** AD?

9 IN 1971, WHICH **ARSENAL** DEFENDER WAS PICTURED IN THE TABLOIDS MODELLING A FLAT CAP AND A **"SMOKING DRESS"** FROM THE FLAMBOYANT **MR. FISH** FASHION HOUSE?

CHARLIE IS MY DARLING

CHARLIE BUCHAN BEGAN HIS CAREER AS AN AMATEUR WITH *WOOLWICH ARSENAL* IN 1909. HE WON A LEAGUE TITLE AND LOST THE FA CUP FINAL WITH *SUNDERLAND* BEFORE SERVING WITH THE GRENADIER GUARDS AND THEN THE SHERWOOD FORESTERS DURING THE FIRST WORLD WAR, RISING TO THE RANK OF SECOND LIEUTENANT. RESUMING HIS CAREER ON WEARSIDE, HE WAS THE FIRST DIVISION'S TOP SCORER IN THE 1922-23 SEASON. HE LEFT *SUNDERLAND* FOR *ARSENAL* IN 1925, HIS 209 GOALS MAKING HIM *SUNDERLAND'S* ALL-TIME RECORD LEAGUE GOALSCORER. THE GOALS CONTINUED TO FLOW AT *ARSENAL* AND HE CAPTAINED *THE GUNNERS* TO THEIR FIRST EVER CUP FINAL IN 1927. HE RETIRED THE FOLLOWING YEAR AND BECAME A FOOTBALL JOURNALIST.

WHICH *ARSENAL* PLAYER TOPPED THE TOP FLIGHT SCORING CHART IN:

1   1934-35

2   1947-48

3   1990-91

4   2018-19

UP FOR THE CUP

THE 1936 FA CUP FINAL PITTED FIRST DIVISION **ARSENAL** AGAINST
SECOND DIVISION **SHEFFIELD UNITED.** IT WAS **ARSENAL'S** SECOND
FA CUP FINAL, HAVING WON THE TROPHY SIX YEARS EARLIER. A MEDIA
BAN BY THE STADIUM'S BOSSES PROMPTED REPORTERS TO FLY ABOVE
WEMBLEY IN AUTOGYROS TO VIEW THE MATCH AND THE BBC INTRODUCED
COMMENTATORS FOR THE FIRST TIME DURING THE LIVE BROADCAST.
THE GAME WAS WON BY A SINGLE GOAL FROM **TED DRAKE**, WHO WAS
RETURNING FROM AN INJURY LAY-OFF, 16 MINUTES FROM FULL-TIME. IT
WAS **SHEFFIELD UNITED'S** LAST APPEARANCE IN AN FA CUP FINAL.

WHO SCORED THE **ARSENAL** GOALS IN THESE FA CUP FINAL WINS?

1   1930: 2-0 V **HUDDERSFIELD TOWN**

2   1950: 2-0 V **LIVERPOOL**

3   1971: 2-1 V **LIVERPOOL**

4   1979: 3-2 V **MANCHESTER UNITED**

5   1993: 1-1 V **SHEFFIELD WEDNESDAY**
REPLAY: 2-1

6   1998: 2-0 V **NEWCASTLE UNITED**

7   2002: 2-0 V **CHELSEA**

8   2003: 1-0 V **SOUTHAMPTON**

9   2014: 3-2 V **HULL CITY**

10   2015: 4-0 V **ASTON VILLA**

11   2017: 2-1 V **CHELSEA**

12   2020: 2-1 V **CHELSEA**

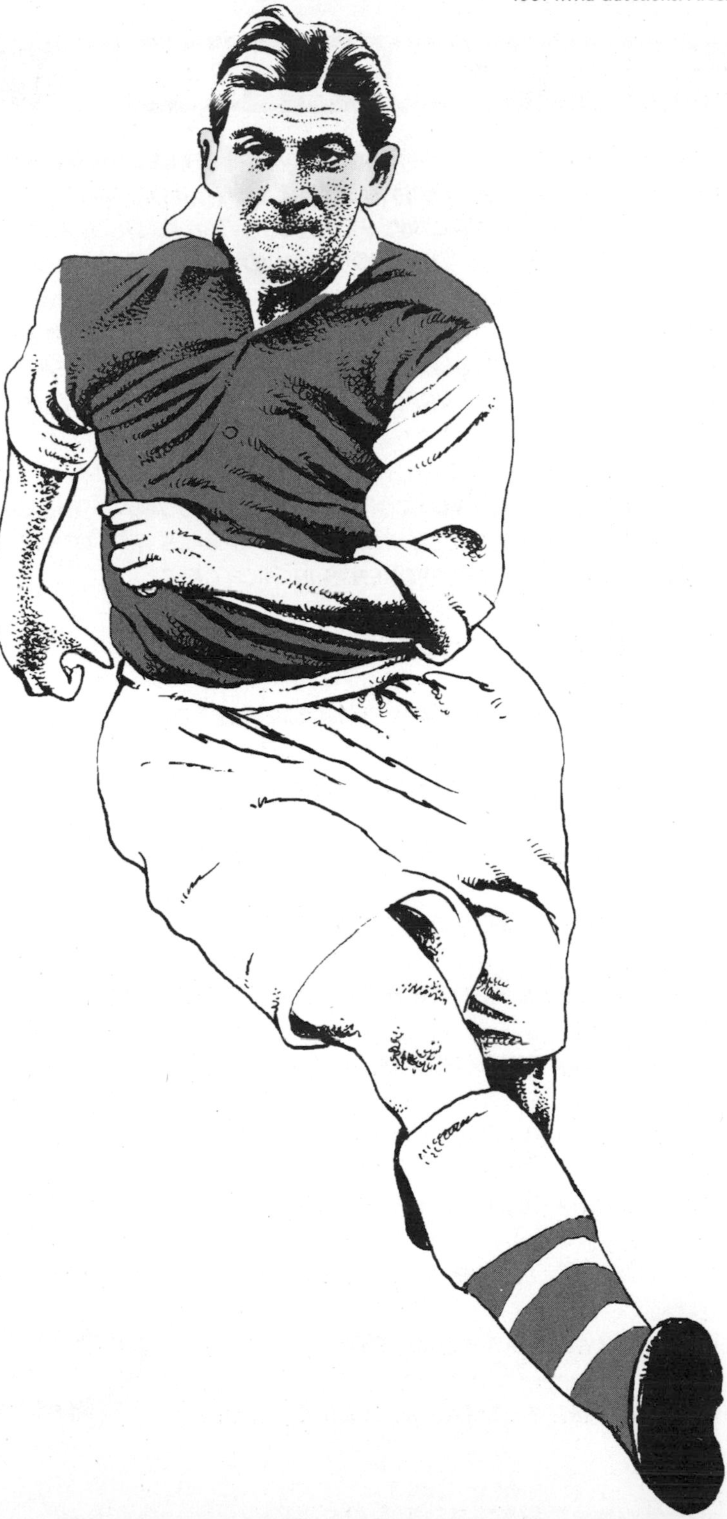

POT COLLECTORS

IN A CAREER THAT SAW HIM PLAY FOR NIGERIAN TEAM *IWUANYANWU NATIONALE*, DUTCH SIDE *AJAX*, *INTERNAZIONALE* OF ITALY, AND ENGLISH CLUBS *ARSENAL*, *WEST BROMWICH ALBION* AND *PORTSMOUTH*, *NIGERIA* INTERNATIONAL *NWANKWO KANU* WON THE PREMIER LEAGUE, FA CUP, CHAMPIONS LEAGUE, UEFA CUP, AN OLYMPIC GOLD MEDAL AND LEAGUE TITLES IN NIGERIA AND THE NETHERLANDS. TWICE NAMED AFRICAN FOOTBALLER OF THE YEAR, HE WON THE FA CUP THREE TIMES -- TWICE WITH *ARSENAL* AND ONCE WITH *PORTSMOUTH*.

HIS THIRD FA CUP MEDAL CAME WITH *PORTSMOUTH'S* 1-0 WIN OVER *CARDIFF CITY* IN 2008, *KANU* SCORING THE ONLY GOAL OF THE GAME. THE FOLLOWING *GUNNERS* ALSO WON FA CUP MEDALS WITH OTHER CLUBS ... BUT WHO WERE THE OPPONENTS IN EACH CASE?

1 2018: *WILLIAN* WITH *CHELSEA*

2 1985: *FRANK STAPLETON* WITH *MANCHESTER UNITED*

3 1970: *JOHN HOLLINS* WITH *CHELSEA*

4 1983: *FRANK STAPLETON* WITH *MANCHESTER UNITED*

5 2010: *NICOLAS ANELKA* WITH *CHELSEA*

6 2004: *MIKAËL SILVESTRE* WITH *MANCHESTER UNITED*

7 1978: *PAUL MARINER* WITH *IPSWICH TOWN*

8 1975: *BOBBY GOULD* WITH *WEST HAM UNITED*

9 2007: *ASHLEY COLE* WITH *CHELSEA*

10 1995: *ANDERS LIMPAR* WITH *EVERTON*

11 2012: *PETR ČECH* WITH *CHELSEA*

12 1992: *MICHAEL THOMAS* WITH *LIVERPOOL*

13 1967: *PAT JENNINGS* WITH *TOTTENHAM HOTSPUR*

14 1960: *EDDIE CLAMP* WITH *WOLVERHAMPTON WANDERERS*

15 2011: *PATRICK VIEIRA* WITH *MANCHESTER CITY*

16 1965: *GEOFF STRONG* WITH *LIVERPOOL*

17 1963: *DAVID HERD* WITH *MANCHESTER UNITED*

SUKERMAN!

CROATIA'S ALL-TIME LEADING GOALSCORER, *DAVOR ŠUKER* SCORED 45 GOALS IN 69 INTERNATIONAL APPEARANCES. PRIOR TO THE FORMATION OF THE *CROATIA* NATIONAL TEAM, HE HAD BEEN CAPPED TWICE BY YUGOSLAVIA. HAVING WON BOTH THE GOLDEN BOOT AND GOLDEN PLAYER AWARDS AT THE UEFA EUROPEAN UNDER-21 CHAMPIONSHIP, HE WAS OUTSTANDING AT THE 1998 WORLD CUP, WINNING THE GOLDEN SHOE AND THE SILVER BALL. AFTER RETIRING FROM PLAYING, *ŠUKER* SERVED FOR NINE YEARS AS PRESIDENT OF THE *CROATIA FOOTBALL FEDERATION*.

1 HAVING LAUNCHED HIS CAREER WITH HOMETOWN CLUB *OSIJEK*, HE SPENT TWO SEASONS WITH *DINAMO ZAGREB* BEFORE JOINING WHICH SPANISH CLUB IN 1991?

2 HIS GOALSCORING EXPLOITS EARNED HIM A MOVE TO SPANISH GIANTS *REAL MADRID* IN 1996, WHERE HE WON LA LIGA IN HIS DEBUT SEASON PLAYING UNDER WHICH ITALIAN COACH?

3 IN HIS SECOND SEASON WITH *"LOS BLANCOS"*, *ŠUKER* WON A UEFA CHAMPIONS LEAGUE PLAYING UNDER WHICH GERMAN COACH?

4 WHO DID *REAL MADRID* BEAT 1-0 IN THE 1998 UEFA CHAMPIONS LEAGUE FINAL, WHICH WAS PLAYED IN AMSTERDAM THAT YEAR?

5 *ŠUKER* SCORED SIX GOALS AT THE 1998 WORLD CUP TO WIN THE GOLDEN SHOE. HE ALSO WON THE SILVER BALL AS THE TOURNAMENT'S SECOND-BEST PLAYER -- WHICH *BRAZIL* STAR WON THE GOLDEN BALL?

6 NAME THE BRITISH MANAGER WHO WAS IN CHARGE OF *REAL MADRID* WHEN *ŠUKER* LEFT TO JOIN *ARSENAL* IN 1999.

7 *ŠUKER* WAS ONE OF THE PLAYERS WHO MISSED A PENALTY AS WHICH TEAM BEAT *THE GUNNERS* IN A SHOOT-OUT TO WIN THE 2000 UEFA CUP FINAL?

8 WHO WAS THE MANAGER WHO SIGNED *ŠUKER* TO *WEST HAM UNITED* IN 2000?

KNOW HOWE?

CAPPED 23 TIMES BY *ENGLAND*, FOR WHOM HE PLAYED AT THE 1958 WORLD CUP, *DON HOWE* BECAME PART OF THE NATIONAL TEAM'S COACHING STAFF UNDER *RON GREENWOOD* IN 1981. HE CONTINUED TO WORK FOR *"THE THREE LIONS"* UNDER *BOBBY ROBSON* AND WAS ASSISTANT MANAGER TO *TERRY VENABLES*.

1   *HOWE* BEGAN HIS CAREER AT *WEST BROMWICH ALBION*, WHERE HE PLAYED UNDER WHICH LEGENDARY ENGLISH MANAGER WHO WON HONOURS WITH *AJAX* AND *BARCELONA?*

2   AFTER PLAYING 379 TIMES FOR *THE BAGGIES*, HE JOINED *ARSENAL* IN 1964. WHO WAS THE MANAGER, A FORMER *ENGLAND* TEAMMATE, WHO SIGNED HOWE TO *THE GUNNERS?*

3   A BROKEN LEG EFFECTIVELY ENDED *HOWE'S* PLAYING CAREER, FOLLOWING WHICH HE JOINED THE *ARSENAL* BACKROOM STAFF UNDER *BERTIE MEE*. *HOWE* WAS APPOINTED FIRST TEAM COACH IN 1967 AFTER WHOSE DEPARTURE TO MANAGE *CHELSEA?*

4   *HOWE* HELPED *ARSENAL* ACHIEVE A 4-3 AGGREGATE VICTORY OVER WHICH TEAM TO WIN THE 1970 INTER-CITIES FAIRS CUP?

5   AFTER COACHING THE *ARSENAL* TEAM THAT WON THE DOUBLE IN 1971, *HOWE* LEFT TO TAKE THE REINS AT WHICH CLUB?

6   *HOWE* WAS SUBSEQUENTLY ASSISTANT MANAGER TO *JIMMY ARMFIELD* AT WHICH CLUB?

7   HE WAS APPOINTED MANAGER OF WHICH TURKISH CLUB IN 1975?

8   RETURNING TO *ARSENAL*, *HOWE* WAS ASSISTANT TO WHICH MANAGER, SUBSEQUENTLY SUCCEEDING HIM AS BOSS?

9   *HOWE* WAS ASSISTANT TO WHICH FORMER *ARSENAL* PLAYER AT *WIMBLEDON*, HELPING THE CLUB WIN THE FA CUP?

10   *HOWE* MANAGED WHICH LONDON CLUB BETWEEN 1989 AND 1991?

11   HE ASSISTED AND THEN SUCCEEDED WHICH FORMER ENGLAND INTERNATIONAL AS MANAGER OF *COVENTRY CITY?*

12   HE ENDED HIS COACHING CAREER BACK AT *ARSENAL*, WHERE HE OVERSAW FA YOUTH CUP WINS IN 2000 AND 2001. WHICH MEMBER OF THE 2000 TEAM WAS SOLD TO *COVENTRY CITY* AFTER THROWING HIS SHIRT AT *HOWE* WHEN HE WAS SUBSTITUTED IN A GAME ... AND WENT ON TO PLAY FOR *WOLVES*, *QPR* AND MORE, WINNING AN *ENGLAND* CAP WHILE PLAYING WITH *CARDIFF CITY?*

MADRIDISTAS

HAVING IRKED A SECTION OF **GUNNERS** SUPPORT BY LEAVING FOR NEWLY CASH-RICH **MANCHESTER CITY** -- AND COMPOUNDED MATTERS WITH AN INFAMOUS GOAL CELEBRATION IN FRONT OF THE **ARSENAL** SUPPORTERS AT **THE ETIHAD** -- **EMMANUEL ADEBAYOR** RUBBED SALT IN THE WOUND BY SIGNING FOR **SPURS** IN 2012. IN BETWEEN, A LOAN SPELL AT **REAL MADRID** YIELDED A COPA DEL REY MEDAL.

IDENTIFY THESE **GUNNERS** WHO ALSO PLAYED FOR **LOS BLANCOS**:

1 NORWEGIAN WHO JOINED **ARSENAL** FROM **REAL MADRID** IN 2021.

2 WORLD CUP-WINNING, FIVE-TIME GERMAN FOOTBALLER OF THE YEAR SIGNED TO **ARSENAL** FROM **REAL MADRID** IN 2013.

3 FRENCH WORLD CUP WINNER WHO WON LEAGUE TITLES WITH **ARSENAL, FENERBAHÇE, CHELSEA** AND **JUVENTUS**, AND THE CHAMPIONS LEAGUE IN HIS ONE SEASON WITH **REAL MADRID**.

4 TWO-TIME COPA AMÉRICA WINNER WITH **BRAZIL**, A STRIKER WHO WON A LEAGUE TITLE WITH **REAL MADRID** IN 2007 AFTER A PERIOD ON LOAN WITH **ARSENAL**.

5 **SPAIN** INTERNATIONAL WHO WON HONOURS WITH **REAL BETIS** AND **REAL MADRID**, HE JOINED **ARSENAL** IN 2019 AND WON THE FA CUP IN HIS FIRST SEASON. HE WON A SILVER MEDAL WITH **SPAIN** AT THE 2020 OLYMPICS.

6 LEAGUE AND CHAMPIONS LEAGUE WINNER WITH **REAL MADRID**, 1998 WORLD CUP GOLDEN SHOE WINNER WHO JOINED **ARSENAL** IN 1999.

THE ITALIAN JOBS

DAVID PLATT'S PERFORMANCES FOR **ENGLAND** AT THE 1990 WORLD CUP EARNED HIM A MOVE FROM **ASTON VILLA** TO **BARI** IN 1991. IT WAS THE FIRST OF THREE CLUBS HE WOULD PLAY FOR IN ITALY. WHILE AT **BARI**, HE WAS PURSUED BY **ROBERTO MANCINI**, WHO WAS KEEN TO HAVE **PLATT** PLAY ALONGSIDE HIM AT **SAMPDORIA**. **PLATT** WASN'T PERSUADED AND THE FOLLOWING YEAR, MOVED TO **JUVENTUS**. UNDETERRED, **MANCINI** PHONED HIM CONSTANTLY AND IN 1993, WHEN THINGS HADN'T PANNED OUT IN TURIN, **PLATT** SIGNED FOR **SAMPDORIA**, STAYING FOR TWO SEASONS BEFORE JOINING **ARSENAL**.

WHICH ITALIAN CLUBS DID THE FOLLOWING **GUNNERS** PLAY FOR?

1 **ASHLEY COLE** 2014-16

2 **JOE BAKER** 1961-62

3 **DAVID OSPINA** 2018-

4 **BACARY SAGNA** 2018-

5 **SOKRATIS PAPASTATHOPOULOS** 2008-10 BEFORE JOINING **AC MILAN**

6 **HENRIKH MKHITARYAN** 2019-

7 **ANDERS LIMPAR** 1989-90

8 **JAY BOTHROYD** 2003-05

9 **THOMAS VERMAELEN** 2016-17

10 **ALEXIS SÁNCHEZ** 2006-11

11 **JOEL CAMPBELL** 2018-20

12 **WOJCIECH SZCZĘSNY** 2015-17 BEFORE JOINING **JUVENTUS**

THE OLD FIRM

HAVING PLAYED ON LOAN FROM **BARCELONA** AT **PARIS SAINT-GERMAIN**, **MIKEL ARTETA** SPENT TWO SEASONS AT **RANGERS**, WHERE HE WON A LEAGUE AND CUP DOUBLE IN 2003. A BRIEF SPELL AT **REAL SOCIEDAD** WAS FOLLOWED BY EIGHT SEASONS WITH **EVERTON**, BEFORE HE SIGNED FOR **THE GUNNERS** IN 2011. HE WON TWO FA CUPS WITH **ARSENAL** BEFORE HANGING UP HIS BOOTS IN 2016 TO COACH UNDER **PEP GUARDIOLA** AT **MANCHESTER CITY**.

NAME THESE **GUNNERS** WHO HAVE PLAYED FOR **RANGERS** OR **CELTIC**, THE GLASGOW CLUBS KNOWN COLLECTIVELY AS **"THE OLD FIRM"**.

1 **SCOTLAND** INTERNATIONAL FULL-BACK WHO WON FOUR CONSECUTIVE LEAGUE TITLES, TWO SCOTTISH CUPS AND TWO LEAGUE CUPS -- INCLUDING THE TREBLE IN 2018 -- BEFORE JOINING **ARSENAL** FROM **CELTIC** FOR A RECORD £25 MILLION IN 2019.

2 SWISS CENTRAL DEFENDER WHOSE CLUBS INCLUDE **ARSENAL, AC MILAN, EVERTON, FULHAM, GRASSHOPPERS** AND **RANGERS**.

3 CAPPED 106 TIMES BY **NETHERLANDS**, HE WON A TREBLE AND A DOUBLE WITH **RANGERS** BEFORE JOINING **ARSENAL** IN 2001. HE WON THE PREMIER LEAGUE IN HIS DEBUT SEASON, THEN MOVED TO **BARCELONA** IN 2003, WITH WHOM HE WON TWO LEAGUE TITLES AND THE UEFA CHAMPIONS LEAGUE.

4 **SCOTLAND** STRIKER SIGNED FROM **CELTIC** IN 1983, HE SCORED BOTH GOALS IN **ARSENAL'S** WIN OVER **LIVERPOOL** IN THE 1987 LEAGUE CUP FINAL, BEFORE HEADING BACK TO SCOTLAND, WHERE HE PLAYED FOR **ABERDEEN**, HAD A SECOND SPELL WITH **CELTIC** AND ENDED HIS PLAYING DAYS AT **CLYDE**.

5 **ARSENAL** GOALSCORING LEGEND, **ENGLAND** STRIKER WHO FOLLOWED HIS **GUNNER** GLORY DAYS WITH SPELLS AT **WEST HAM UNITED, CELTIC** AND **BURNLEY**.

6 **IVORY COAST** DEFENDER WHO WON LEAGUE TITLES WITH **ARSENAL, MANCHESTER CITY** AND **CELTIC** AND REACHED LEAGUE CUP AND EUROPA LEAGUE FINALS WITH **LIVERPOOL**.

7 A GOALSCORING SENSATION WITH *EVERTON*, HE JOINED *ARSENAL* IN 2001 BUT THE MOVE DIDN'T WORK OUT. HE SUBSEQUENTLY RETURNED BRIEFLY TO *"THE TOFFEES"* BEFORE PLAYING FOR *CHARLTON ATHLETIC*, *RANGERS*, *BLACKBURN ROVERS*, *IPSWICH TOWN*, *SHEFFIELD WEDNESDAY* AND MORE.

8 HE LAUNCHED HIS CAREER AT *CELTIC* AFTER THE SECOND WORLD WAR, PLAYED FOR *PRESTON NORTH END*, *ARSENAL* AND *CHELSEA*, BEFORE EMBARKING ON A COLOURFUL AND VERY SUCCESSFUL CAREER IN MANAGEMENT.

9 *SWEDEN* STRIKER WHO WON TWO LEAGUE TITLES AND THREE FA CUPS WITH *ARSENAL* IN THE EARLY 2000S, BEFORE PLAYING FOR *WEST HAM UNITED*, *CELTIC* AND TEAMS IN THE STATES, JAPAN AND INDIA.

10 HAVING WON LEAGUE AND LEAGUE CUP HONOURS WITH *ARSENAL* IN THE 1980S, WINGER WHO WENT ON TO PLAY FOR *CELTIC*, *WIMBLEDON*, *SWANSEA CITY* AND MORE.

CHIPPY'S RUN

LIAM BRADY WAS KNOWN AT **ARSENAL** AS **"CHIPPY".** THE SOUBRIQUET HAD NOTHING TO DO WITH HIS ABILITY TO CLIP A THROUGH PASS AND WAS NOT A SLIGHT ON HIS TEMPERAMENT -- WHEN HE JOINED THE CLUB, HIS MOTHER TOLD THE CHIEF SCOUT ABOUT THE TEENAGER'S FONDNESS FOR DEEP-FRIED SPUDS AND THE NICKNAME WAS BORN! ONE OF THE ALL-TIME **GUNNER** GREATS, HE WAS NAMED **ARSENAL** PLAYER OF THE YEAR THREE TIMES.

1 BRADY WAS OUTSTANDING IN THE **TERRY NEILL** SIDE THAT REACHED THREE CONSECUTIVE FA CUP FINALS, WINNING ONCE. HE WAS ALSO IN THE SIDE THAT LOST TO WHICH TEAM IN THE 1980 EUROPEAN CUP WINNERS' CUP FINAL?

2 BRADY WON TWO SERIE A TITLES WITH **JUVENTUS** BEFORE THE ARRIVAL OF WHICH SUPERSTAR FRENCH MIDFIELDER PROMPTED HIS MOVE TO **SAMPDORIA?**

3 AT **SAMPDORIA**, HE PLAYED IN THE SAME TEAM AS WHICH **ENGLAND** STRIKER BETWEEN 1982 AND 1984?

4 HIS NEXT MOVE TOOK HIM TO **INTERNAZIONALE**, WHERE HE PLAYED ALONGSIDE WHICH LEGENDARY GERMAN STRIKER?

5 BRADY SPENT THE 1986-87 SEASON PLAYING FOR WHICH ITALIAN TEAM WHOSE NICKNAME IS **"THE WOODPECKERS"?**

6 WHO WAS THE **WEST HAM UNITED** MANAGER WHO BROUGHT **BRADY** BACK TO LONDON IN 1987?

7 HE MADE HIS **REPUBLIC OF IRELAND** DEBUT IN OCTOBER, 1974 AND WON THE LAST OF HIS 72 CAPS IN 1990. NAME THE THREE MANAGERS UNDER WHOM HE PLAYED.

8 IN 1991, **BRADY** SUCCEEDED WHICH FORMER **SCOTLAND** INTERNATIONAL DEFENDER AS MANAGER OF **CELTIC?**

9 TWO YEARS LATER, HE SUCCEEDED **BARRY LLOYD** AS MANAGER OF WHICH CLUB?

10 **BRADY** WAS ASSISTANT MANAGER OF THE **REPUBLIC OF IRELAND,** WORKING UNDER WHICH MANAGER WHO HAD COACHED HIM AT **JUVENTUS?**

PFA POTY

ARSENAL'S TOP SCORER IN THE 1998-99 SEASON, HIS FORM EARNED **NICOLAS ANELKA** THE PFA YOUNG PLAYER OF THE YEAR AWARD. EACH SEASON, MEMBERS OF THE PROFESSIONAL FOOTBALLERS' ASSOCIATION -- THE FOOTBALLERS' TRADE UNION -- VOTE FOR THEIR PLAYER OF THE YEAR AND YOUNG PLAYER OF THE YEAR. IDENTIFY THE FOLLOWING **GUNNERS** WHO HAVE BEEN HONOURED, EITHER AS AN **ARSENAL** PLAYER OR DURING THEIR TIME AT ANOTHER CLUB:

1 1975-76 POTY: **TOTTENHAM HOTSPUR** GOALKEEPER.

2 1977-78 YOUNG POTY: **NOTTINGHAM FOREST** STRIKER.

3 1978-79 POTY: **REPUBLIC OF IRELAND** MIDFIELDER, THE FIRST "FOREIGN" PLAYER TO WIN THE AWARD.

4 1986-87 POTY: **TOTTENHAM HOTSPUR** STRIKER.

5 1987-88 YOUNG POTY: WOULD SPEND 19 YEARS AT **ARSENAL**.

6 1988-89 YOUNG POTY: MIDFIELDER WHO WON NUMEROUS HONOURS WITH **THE GUNNERS** AND LATER WON HONOURS WITH **ASTON VILLA** AND **PORTSMOUTH**.

7 1989-90 POTY: **ENGLAND** AND **ASTON VILLA** MIDFIELDER.

8 1993-94 YOUNG POTY: **NEWCASTLE UNITED** GOALGETTER.

9 1997-98 POTY: DUTCH FORWARD.

10 2002-03 AND 2003-04 POTY: **FRANCE** AND **ARSENAL** LEGEND.

11 2007-08 YOUNG POTY: SPANISH MIDFIELDER.

12 2010-11 YOUNG POTY: **ENGLAND** MIDFIELDER WHOSE SUBSEQUENT CLUBS INCLUDE **WEST HAM UNITED** AND **BOURNEMOUTH**.

13 2011-12 POTY: ALL-TIME TOP **NETHERLANDS** GOALSCORER.

PORTUGUESE GEEZERS

HAVING WON THE 2019 PORTUGUESE SUPER CUP WITH **BENFICA**, LEFT-BACK **NUNO TAVARES** SIGNED FOR **ARSENAL** IN 2021. IDENTIFY THESE OTHER **GUNNERS** WITH PORTUGUESE CONNECTIONS.

1 **SWEDEN** INTERNATIONAL MIDFIELDER WHO WON HONOURS WITH **MALMÖ**, HE JOINED **ARSENAL** FROM **BENFICA** IN 1994, HAVING WON TWO LEAGUE TITLES AND THE TAÇA DE PORTUGAL -- THE CUP OF PORTUGAL -- WITH THE LISBON TEAM. HE WENT ON TO WIN HONOURS WITH **FIORENTINA** AND **VALENCIA** BEFORE ENDING HIS PLAYING DAYS WITH A FOUR-YEAR STINT AT **SUNDERLAND**.

2 BORN IN GERMANY BUT RAISED IN PORTUGAL, A RIGHT-BACK WHO WON THE TAÇA DE PORTUGAL WITH BOTH **ACADÉMICA** AND **SPORTING CP** BEFORE JOINING **SOUTHAMPTON** IN 2015. A **PORTUGAL** INTERNATIONAL, HE PLAYED FOR **INTERNAZIONALE** ON LOAN BEFORE HIS LOAN MOVE TO **ARSENAL** WAS MADE PERMANENT IN 2020.

3 HAVING LAUNCHED HIS SENIOR CAREER AT **ARSENAL** -- WHO LOANED HIM OUT TO **CRYSTAL PALACE** IN 2010 -- HIS CLUBS HAVE INCLUDED **BENFICA, ESPANYOL, FULHAM** AND **BRAGA**.

4 **ENGLAND** MIDFIELDER WHO WON TWO LEAGUE TITLES AND THE LEAGUE CUP WITH **ARSENAL**, AND THE LEAGUE CUP AND FA CUP WITH **LIVERPOOL**, BEFORE JOINING **GRAEME SOUNESS** AT **BENFICA** IN 1998. HE ENDED HIS CAREER WITH A SPELL AT **WIMBLEDON** BEFORE RETIRING IN 2001.

5 DUTCH WINGER, CAPPED FOUR TIMES BY THE **NETHERLANDS**, HE WAS LOANED OUT TO **BENFICA** BY **ARSENAL** IN 1998. HE WENT ON TO PLAY IN CHINA, HUNGARY AND FOR A NUMBER OF DUTCH SIDES.

6 **PORTUGAL** INTERNATIONAL MIDFIELDER, HE JOINED **ARSENAL** FROM **SPORTING CP** IN 1997 AND WON A LEAGUE TITLE THE FOLLOWING YEAR, BEFORE HIS CAREER TOOK HIM TO **SOUTHAMPTON, FULHAM, WEST HAM UNITED**, AND TEAMS IN GREECE AND SOUTH AFRICA, BEFORE HE ENDED HIS PLAYING DAYS WITH A BRIEF SOJOURN AT **CHESTERFIELD**.

THERE'S NO BUSINESS LIKE SHOW BUSINESS

AN APPRENTICE GAS METER READER WHO PLAYED HIS FOOTBALL FOR **SOUTHAMPTON GASWORKS** AND **WINCHESTER CITY**, **TED DRAKE** SIGNED PROFESSIONAL FORMS WITH **SOUTHAMPTON** IN 1931. HIS GOALSCORING FORM PROMPTED **ARSENAL** TO PAY £6,500 TO ACQUIRE HIS SERVICES IN 1934 -- ALTHOUGH THE CASH-STRAPPED **SAINTS** WERE SAID TO HAVE BEEN LEFT WITH JUST £250 AFTER DEBTS HAD BEEN PAID!

THE INVESTMENT PAID OFF HANDSOMELY. IN HIS FIRST FULL SEASON WITH **THE GUNNERS** HE HIT A CLUB RECORD 44 GOALS, 42 OF THEM IN THE LEAGUE TO PROPEL **ARSENAL** TO THE TITLE. THE FOLLOWING SEASON, HE SCORED SEVEN GOALS IN ONE LEAGUE GAME AND HIT THE WINNER IN THE FA CUP FINAL. HE ADDED ANOTHER LEAGUE TITLE TO HIS MEDAL HAUL IN 1938. BUT FOR THE SECOND WORLD WAR AND THE INJURY THAT ENDED HIS CAREER SOON AFTER FOOTBALL RESUMED, HE WOULD CERTAINLY HAVE ADDED GREATLY TO HIS TALLY OF 139 GOALS IN 184 GAMES.

DRAKE, ALONG WITH FELLOW GUNNERS INCLUDING **GEORGE SWINDIN**, **CLIFF BASTIN** AND **EDDIE HAPGOOD**, APPEARED IN THE 1939 CRIME THRILLER **"THE ARSENAL STADIUM MYSTERY"**. MANAGER **GEORGE ALLISON** HAD A SPEAKING PART AND DELIVERED THE LINE: **"IT'S ONE-NIL TO THE ARSENAL. THAT'S THE WAY WE LIKE IT"**.

IDENTIFY THESE OTHER **ARSENAL** AND THESPIAN LINKS:

1 WHICH **ARSENAL** AND **ENGLAND** FULL-BACK HAD A CAMEO ROLE IN A 1973 EPISODE OF THE SITCOM **"ON THE BUSES"**?

2 WHICH FORMER **ARSENAL** AND **ENGLAND** FULL-BACK TEAMED UP WITH **RIO FERDINAND** TO EXECUTIVE PRODUCE THE 2009 FILM **"DEAD MAN RUNNING"**, WHICH STARRED RAPPER **50 CENT**, **BRENDA BLETHYN**, **DANNY DYER** AND MORE?

3 WHICH **ARSENAL**, **TOTTENHAM HOTSPUR** AND **PORTSMOUTH** DEFENDER HAD A CAMEO ON THE DRAMA SERIES **"FOOTBALLERS' WIVES"**, WHICH RAN ON ITV FROM 2002 TO 2006?

4 ACTOR *PATRICK ROBINSON -- MARTIN "ASH" ASHFORD* IN THE LONG-RUNNING BRITISH MEDICAL DRAMA SERIES *"CASUALTY"* -- IS THE COUSIN OF WHICH *ARSENAL* AND *ENGLAND* STRIKER?

5 WHICH *ARSENAL* AND *ENGLAND* CENTRE-HALF APPEARED WITH *CHELSEA'S GIANFRANCO ZOLA* IN AN EPISODE OF THE *NICKELODEON* TEEN SITCOM *"RENFORD REJECTS"*?

6 ON WHICH POPULAR CHILDREN'S DRAMA DID *LUÍS BOA MORTE* MAKE A CAMEO APPEARANCE IN 1999, PRESENTING A TROPHY TO THE WINNERS OF A SCHOOL FOOTBALL MATCH?

7 WHICH *ARSENAL* AND *ENGLAND* STAR APPEARED OPPOSITE *DIANA DORS* AND *THORA HIRD* IN THE 1953 FILM *"THE GREAT GAME"*?

NOT FROM ROUND HERE

CAPPED 65 TIMES BY **MOROCCO, MAROUANE CHAMAKH** PLAYED IN THE TEAM THAT FINISHED RUNNERS-UP AT THE 2004 AFRICA CUP OF NATIONS.

WHICH COUNTRY CAPPED THE FOLLOWING ARSENAL PLAYERS?

1 *GLEN KAMARA*

2 *PIERRE-EMERICK AUBAMEYANG*

3 *ISMAËL BENNACER*

4 *OLEG LUZHNY*

5 *IGORS STEPANOVS*

6 *JERNADE MEADE*

7 *ALEXANDER HLEB*

8 *NICO YENNARIS* AKA *LI KE*

9 *VLADIMIR PETROVIĆ*

10 *PARK CHU-YOUNG*

11 *LUCAS TORREIRA*

12 *KABA DIAWARA*

13 *ALEXIS SÁNCHEZ*

14 *DAVID OSPINA*

15 *ARMAND TRAORÉ*

16 *THOMAS PARTEY*

17 *RÚNAR ALEX RÚNARSSON*

PLATT'S THE WAY TO DO IT

A WORLD CUP HERO WITH **ENGLAND** AT THE 1990 WORLD CUP, **DAVID PLATT** WON HONOURS WITH **ASTON VILLA**, **JUVENTUS** AND **SAMPDORIA**, AND WAS A LEAGUE AND FA CUP DOUBLE WINNER WITH **ARSENAL** IN 1998. UPON RETIRING, HE EMBARKED ON A COACHING CAREER THAT HAS SEEN HIM MANAGE TEAMS IN HIS OWN RIGHT AND ACT AS AN ASSISTANT AND CONSULTANT.

1 IMMEDIATELY AFTER LEAVING **ARSENAL**, **PLATT** BECAME MANAGER OF WHICH ITALIAN TEAM?

2 HE WAS APPOINTED PLAYER/MANAGER OF WHICH CLUB IN 1999, SUCCEEDING **RON ATKINSON?**

3 IN 2001, HE SUCCEEDED WHICH FORMER **LEEDS UNITED** BOSS AS MANAGER OF THE **ENGLAND U21** TEAM?

4 IN 2015, HE MANAGED WHICH INDIAN SUPER LEAGUE TEAM?

PENSIONERS AND GUNNERS

HAVING WON A LEAGUE TITLE IN FRANCE WITH *MONTPELLIER*, *OLIVIER GIROUD* JOINED *ARSENAL* IN 2012. IN SIX SEASONS WITH *THE GUNNERS* HE WON THREE FA CUPS, BEFORE MOVING TO *CHELSEA* IN EARLY 2018, THE SAME YEAR HE WON THE WORLD CUP WITH *FRANCE*. HE ADDED AN FA CUP, THE EUROPA LEAGUE AND THE UEFA CHAMPIONS LEAGUE TO HIS MEDAL TALLY BEFORE JOINING *AC MILAN* IN 2021.

IDENTIFY THESE *ARSENAL* STARS WHO HAVE PLAYED FOR *CHELSEA:*

1 *FRANCE* DEFENSIVE MIDFIELDER WHO WON THE FA CUP AND LEAGUE CUP WITH *CHELSEA* BEFORE JOINING *ARSENAL* IN 2007. A LACK OF OPPORTUNITIES SAW HIM LEAVE FOR *PORTSMOUTH* AFTER JUST FIVE MONTHS. HE WON THE FA CUP WITH *POMPEY* BEFORE GOING ON TO WIN LEAGUE TITLES WITH *REAL MADRID* AND *PARIS SAINT-GERMAIN*.

2 *CHELSEA* STALWART WHOSE HONOURS INCLUDED THE FA CUP, LEAGUE CUP AND UEFA CUP WINNERS' CUP. HE JOINED *QUEENS PARK RANGERS* IN 1975 AFTER A DOZEN YEARS AT STAMFORD BRIDGE, BEFORE SIGNING FOR *ARSENAL* IN 1979. HE SUBSEQUENTLY PLAYED FOR *CHELSEA* ONCE MORE AND WAS APPOINTED MANAGER IN 1985.

3 COLOURFUL *SCOTLAND* WING-HALF WHO PLAYED FOR *CELTIC*, *PRESTON NORTH END*, *ARSENAL* AND *CHELSEA* BEFORE MANAGING *CHELSEA* IN THE 1960S, *MANCHESTER UNITED* IN THE 1970S AND A HOST OF OTHER CLUBS.

4 ENGLAND FULL-BACK WHOSE CLUBS INCLUDED *ARSENAL*, *CHELSEA*, *ROMA*, *LA GALAXY* AND *DERBY COUNTY*.

5 *ARSENAL*, *LEEDS UNITED*, *MANCHESTER CITY* AND *CHELSEA* MIDFIELDER WHO DIED IN 2001 AT THE AGE OF 33.

6 BRAZILIAN WHO WON MULTIPLE HONOURS WITH *SHAKHTAR DONETSK* AND *CHELSEA* BEFORE JOINING *ARSENAL* IN 2020.

UNDER SPANISH SKIES

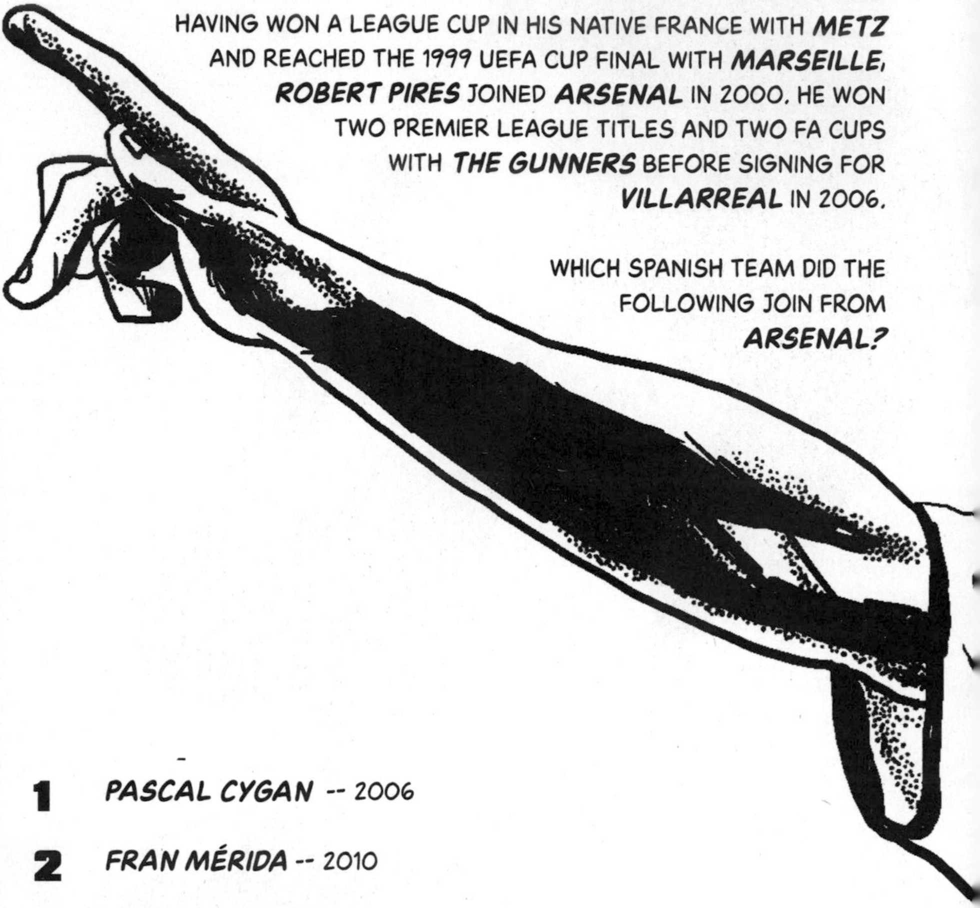

HAVING WON A LEAGUE CUP IN HIS NATIVE FRANCE WITH *METZ* AND REACHED THE 1999 UEFA CUP FINAL WITH *MARSEILLE*, *ROBERT PIRES* JOINED *ARSENAL* IN 2000. HE WON TWO PREMIER LEAGUE TITLES AND TWO FA CUPS WITH *THE GUNNERS* BEFORE SIGNING FOR *VILLARREAL* IN 2006.

WHICH SPANISH TEAM DID THE FOLLOWING JOIN FROM *ARSENAL?*

1 *PASCAL CYGAN* -- 2006

2 *FRAN MÉRIDA* -- 2010

3 *FRANCIS COQUELIN* -- 2018

4 *SANTI CAZORLA* -- 2018

5 *GABRIEL PAULISTA* -- 2017

6 *EDU GASPAR* -- 2005

7 *CARLOS VELA* -- 2012

8 *NACHO MONREAL* -- 2019

9 *SYLVINHO* -- 2001

10 *JOSÉ ANTONIO REYES* -- 2008

11 *KEVIN RICHARDSON* -- 1990

BRIGHTON PEERS

SIGNED TO *BRIGHTON & HOVE ALBION* AS A TEEN IN 2014 AFTER BEING RELEASED BY *SOUTHAMPTON, BEN WHITE* BUILT HIS REPUTATION ON LOAN AT *NEWPORT COUNTY, PETERBOROUGH UNITED* AND *LEEDS UNITED.* HE FINALLY MADE HIS *BRIGHTON* DEBUT IN SEPTEMBER, 2020, AT THE START OF A SEASON WHICH ENDED WITH HIM WINNING HIS FIRST *ENGLAND* CAP, BEFORE REPLACING THE INJURED *TRENT ALEXANDER-ARNOLD* IN THE EUROPEAN CHAMPIONSHIP SQUAD AND THEN INKING HIS £50 MILLION TRANSFER TO *ARSENAL.*

IDENTIFY THESE OTHER *GUNNERS* WITH LINKS TO *"THE SEAGULLS"*:

1 ENGLAND FORWARD WHO WON HONOURS WITH *MANCHESTER UNITED* AND *ARSENAL,* HAD LOAN SPELLS WITH *PRESTON NORTH END* AND SUNDERLAND, AND JOINED *BRIGHTON & HOVE ALBION* FROM *WATFORD* IN 2020.

2 IRISH GOALGETTER WHO WON FA CUPS WITH *ARSENAL* AND *MANCHESTER UNITED,* PLAYED FOR A NUMBER OF OTHER CLUBS IN ENGLAND, THE NETHERLANDS, BELGIUM AND FRANCE, BEFORE ENDING HIS PLAYING DAYS AT *BRIGHTON* IN THE MID-1990S.

3 NORTHERN IRELAND RIGHT-BACK WHO SPENT SIX YEARS WITH THE GUNNERS BEFORE SIGNING FOR *BRIGHTON* IN 1965, HE LATER COACHED EXTENSIVELY IN DENMARK.

4 CENTRE-BACK LOANED BY *THE GUNNERS* TO BRIGHTON AS A TEEN, HE WAS TRANSFERRED TO *ASTON VILLA* AND *EVERTON* BEFORE RETURNING TO *ARSENAL* IN 1993, WHERE HE WON THREE PREMIER LEAGUES AND THREE FA CUPS -- INCLUDING TWO DOUBLES -- AND THE EUROPEAN CUP WINNERS' CUP. HE LATER PLAYED FOR *LEICESTER CITY* AND *READING.*

5 CHELSEA CAPTAIN WHO LED THEM TO PROMOTION IN 1984, HE SPENT TWO YEARS WITH *CHARLTON ATHLETIC* BEFORE JOINING *ARSENAL* IN 1990. THE MOVE DIDN'T PAN OUT AND HE SUBSEQUENTLY MOVED ON TO *BRIGHTON.*

6   *ARSENAL* AND JUVENTUS GREAT WHO MANAGED *BRIGHTON & HOVE ALBION* BETWEEN 1993 AND 1995.

7   *SCOTLAND* STRIKER WHO STARTED HIS CAREER AT *ARSENAL*, WHERE HE WAS LOANED OUT TO *LUTON TOWN* AND *BRIGHTON*, BEFORE A NOMADIC CAREER THAT INCLUDED TWO SPELLS EACH WITH *MANCHESTER CITY* AND *LEICESTER CITY*, BEFORE HE WAS NAMED *OLDHAM ATHLETIC* PLAYER/MANAGER IN 2010.

8   *NORTHERN IRELAND* LEFT-BACK WHO PLAYED IN *ARSENAL'S* THREE FINALS BETWEEN 1978 AND 1980, AND THE EUROPEAN CUP WINNERS' CUP FINAL, BEFORE JOINING *BRIGHTON* IN 1981.

LEADING BY EXAMPLE

A PRODUCT OF THE *AC MILAN* ACADEMY, *PIERRE-EMERICK AUBAMEYANG* WAS LOANED OUT TO A NUMBER OF CLUBS IN HIS NATIVE FRANCE, INCLUDING *DIJON, LILLE* AND *MONACO*, DURING WHICH TIME HE MADE HIS INTERNATIONAL DEBUT FOR *GABON*. A LOAN MOVE TO *SAINT-ÉTIENNE* WAS MADE PERMANENT IN 2011, *AUBAMEYANG* WINNING THE COUPE DE LA LIGUE BEFORE JOINING *BORUSSIA DORTMUND* IN 2013. IN FIVE SEASONS IN GERMANY HE GAINED CUP HONOURS AND WON BOTH BUNDESLIGA AND AFRICAN PLAYER OF THE YEAR AWARDS. HE SIGNED FOR *ARSENAL* IN EARLY 2018 IN A CLUB RECORD £56 MILLION DEAL. HE CAPTAINED THE TEAM -- AND SCORED BOTH GOALS -- IN THE 2-1 WIN OVER *CHELSEA* IN THE FA CUP FINAL.

FROM WHICH TEAMS WERE THESE 2020 FA CUP WINNERS SIGNED (YOUTH TEAM GRADUATES ARE OMITTED FROM THE LIST):

1 *ROB HOLDING*

2 *DAVID LUIZ*

3 *KIERAN TIERNEY*

4 *DANI CEBALLOS*

5 *GRANIT XHAKA*

6 *NICOLAS PÉPÉ*

7 *ALEXANDRE LACAZETTE*

8 *SOKRATIS PAPASTATHOPOULOS*

9 *SEAD KOLAŠINAC*

10 *LUCAS TORREIRA*

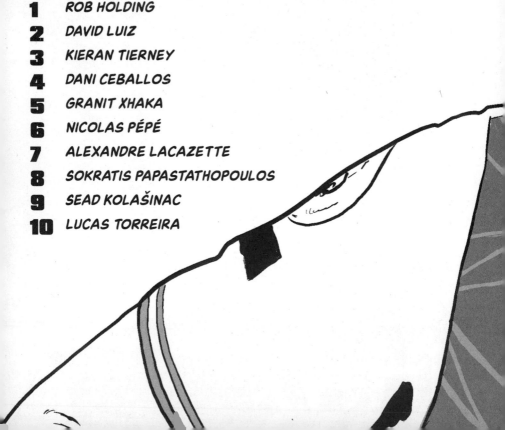

KEEPING UP APPEARANCES

HAVING SPENT 18 SEASONS WITH **THE GUNNERS** -- RACKING UP A CLUB RECORD 722 APPEARANCES -- **REPUBLIC OF IRELAND** CENTRE-BACK **DAVID O'LEARY** PLAYED TWO INJURY-PLAGUED SEASONS WITH **LEEDS UNITED**. HE SUBSEQUENTLY WORKED AS **GEORGE GRAHAM'S** ASSISTANT AT **LEEDS** BEFORE HE WAS APPOINTED MANAGER IN 1998. HE WENT ON TO MANAGE **ASTON VILLA** AND DUBAI'S **AL-AHLI**.

IDENTIFY THESE OTHER LONG-SERVING **GUNNERS** WHO MADE MORE THAN 400 APPEARANCES FOR THE CLUB:

1   669 GAMES: 1983-2002 **ENGLAND** CENTRE-BACK

2   621 GAMES: 1962-1977 WINGER, LATER COACHED THE RESERVES

3   618 GAMES: 1988-2002 **ENGLAND** FULL-BACK

4   584 GAMES: 1987-2000 FULL-BACK SIGNED FROM **WIMBLEDON**

5   564 GAMES: 1990-2003 **ENGLAND** GOALKEEPER

6   528 GAMES: 1967-1980 **NORTHERN IRELAND** RIGHT-BACK

7   501 GAMES: 1965-1977 HARDMAN WHO FELL FOUL OF THE LAW

8   481 GAMES: 1964-1976 **ARSENAL'S** YOUNGEST HAT-TRICK SCORER

9   477 GAMES: 1964-1978 BACK FOUR MAINSTAY OF DOUBLE WINNERS

10   470 GAMES: 1922-1937 **WALES** MIDFIELDER WHO WON THREE LEAGUE TITLES AND THE FA CUP

11   464 GAMES: 1977-1988 **ENGLAND** MIDFIELDER WHOSE COACHING CAREER HAD TO SURVIVE A 1999 JAIL TERM

12   464 GAMES: 1992-2004 NICKNAMED **"THE ROMFORD PELÉ"**

13   449 GAMES: 1985-1986, 1993-2004 **ENGLAND** CENTRAL DEFENDER WHO HAD TWO SPELLS AT THE CLUB

14   447 GAMES: 1980-1994 JAWBREAKING MIDFIELDER

15   440 GAMES: 1927-1939 CAPTAINED **ENGLAND** AND **ARSENAL**

16   425 GAMES: 1986-1997 JOINED RELEGATED **MIDDLESBROUGH**

17   423 GAMES: 1995-2006 THE NON-FLYING DUTCHMAN

18   406 GAMES: 1996-2005 FRENCH WORLD CUP AND EURO WINNER

19   403 GAMES: 1964-1973 SCOTTISH CAPTAIN OF THE DOUBLE WINNERS

"THE BOYS FROM THE MERSEY ..."

MICHAEL THOMAS JOINED ARSENAL AS A 15-YEAR-OLD. THE 1988-89 SEASON SAW HIM MAKE HIS ENGLAND DEBUT AND ENDED WITH HIM SCORING A SENSATIONAL LAST-MINUTE GOAL IN A TITLE-DECIDER AT LIVERPOOL THAT CLINCHED THE CHAMPIONSHIP. HE WON A SECOND TITLE WITH ARSENAL BEFORE JOINING LIVERPOOL IN 1991, WHERE HE WENT ON TO WIN THE LEAGUE CUP AND THE FA CUP.

IDENTIFY THESE OTHER ARSENAL PLAYERS WITH LIVERPOOL LINKS:

1 AUSTRIAN GOALKEEPER WHO WAS DAVID SEAMAN'S DEPUTY AT ARSENAL, GIANLUIGI BUFFON'S AT JUVENTUS AND COVER FOR SIMON JENTZSCH AT FC AUGSBURG, BEFORE RETIRING IN 2017 AFTER A BRIEF SPELL AT LIVERPOOL.

2 SIGNED AS A 15-YEAR-OLD FROM NOTTS COUNTY FOR £2 MILLION, HE MADE HIS ARSENAL DEBUT AT 16 BUT FAILED TO FULFIL EARLY PROMISE AND WENT ON TO PLAY FOR A LENGTHY LIST OF CLUBS, INCLUDING BIRMINGHAM CITY, LIVERPOOL AND STOKE CITY IN A CAREER DOGGED BY POOR DISCIPLINE AND LEGAL WOES.

3 ISRAELI STAR WHO LEFT WEST HAM UNITED FOR LIVERPOOL, WON THE UEFA EUROPA LEAGUE IN 2013 WITH CHELSEA AND SPENT TIME ON LOAN AT ARSENAL AND WEST HAM BEFORE JOINING QUEENS PARK RANGERS.

4 HAVING FORMED A GOALSCORING PARTNERSHIP WITH JOE BAKER IN THE EARLY 1960S, HE WON LEAGUE AND FA CUP HONOURS WITH LIVERPOOL BEFORE ENDING HIS CAREER WITH COVENTRY CITY.

5 CAPPED 120 TIMES BY IVORY COAST, HE WON LEAGUE TITLES WITH ARSENAL AND MANCHESTER CITY, SPENT THREE SEASONS WITH LIVERPOOL AND WON LEAGUE AND CUP HONOURS WITH CELTIC.

6 HAVING SCORED THE GOAL THAT CLINCHED THE LEAGUE AND SET UP **ARSENAL'S** HISTORIC 1971 DOUBLE, HE WON FIVE LEAGUE TITLES, THE LEAGUE CUP, THE UEFA CUP, THE UEFA SUPER CUP AND THREE EUROPEAN CUPS WITH **LIVERPOOL**, THE WELSH CUP WITH **SWANSEA CITY** AND WAS CAPPED 15 TIMES BY **ENGLAND**.

7 GOALKEEPER WHO WON PROMOTION WITH **LIVERPOOL** IN 1962 BEFORE BECOMING **JACK KELSEY'S** SUCCESSOR AT **ARSENAL**, HE LATER PLAYED FOR **ROTHERHAM UNITED** BEFORE SPENDING SIX YEARS WITH **PLYMOUTH ARGYLE**.

8 EURO 2000 WINNER WHO WON HONOURS WITH **ARSENAL**, **REAL MADRID**, **PSG**, **FENERBAHÇE**, **CHELSEA** AND **REAL MADRID** AND PLAYED AT **LIVERPOOL** IN 2001-02.

" ... AND THE THAMES ... "

SITTING BESIDE THE RIVER THAMES, CRAVEN COTTAGE HAS BEEN HOME TO **FULHAM**, LONDON'S OLDEST PROFESSIONAL FOOTBALL CLUB, SINCE 1896. OVER THE YEARS, A NUMBER OF **ARSENAL** PLAYERS HAVE CONTINUED THEIR CAREERS WITH **THE COTTAGERS:**

1   **PHILIPPE SENDEROS** WON THE FA CUP DURING HIS SEVEN SEASONS WITH **ARSENAL** BEFORE JOINING **FULHAM** IN 2010. HE WAS CAPPED 57 TIMES BY WHICH COUNTRY?

2   WHICH **ENGLAND** FULL-BACK AND DEFENSIVE MIDFIELDER WITH A FEARSOME REPUTATION WHO WON THE INTER-CITIES FAIRS CUP IN 1970 AND THE LEAGUE AND FA CUP DOUBLE IN 1971 WITH **ARSENAL** ENDED HIS PLAYING DAYS AT **FULHAM** ALONGSIDE **GEORGE BEST**, **BOBBY MOORE** AND **RODNEY MARSH?**

3   NAME THE GERMAN FULL-BACK WHO WON TWO YOUTH CUPS WITH **ARSENAL** BUT FAILED TO ESTABLISH HIMSELF IN THE SENIOR SIDE. SIGNING FOR **FULHAM** IN 2004, **"THE ELECTRICIAN"** BECAME A FAN FAVOURITE IN HIS FIVE SEASONS AT CRAVEN COTTAGE.

4   WHICH PORTUGUESE WINGER WON THE PREMIER LEAGUE WITH **ARSENAL** IN 1998, THE FIRST DIVISION TITLE WITH **FULHAM** IN 2001 AND PLAYED FOR **SOUTHAMPTON** AND **WEST HAM UNITED?**

5   CAPPED 82 TIMES BY **JAPAN**, WHO SCORED TWICE AT THE 2002 WORLD CUP, BY WHICH TIME HE HAD ALREADY LEFT **ARSENAL** FOR **FULHAM**, WHERE HIS FOUR GOALS IN THE TWO-LEGGED INTERTOTO CUP FINAL WIN OVER **BOLOGNA** MADE HIM A CULT HERO?

6   WHICH **ENGLAND, LUTON TOWN, NEWCASTLE UNITED** AND **ARSENAL** GOALSCORING GREAT PLAYED FOR **FULHAM** EARLY IN HIS CAREER AND RETURNED TO STEER THE CLUB TO A PROMOTION AS MANAGER IN THE EARLY 1980S?

7   WHICH **ARSENAL** YOUTH TEAM PRODUCT, LOANED TO **FULHAM** EARLY IN HIS CAREER, WENT ON TO BECOME PFA YOUNG PLAYER OF THE YEAR, A CHAMPIONS LEAGUE-WINNING, PREMIER LEAGUE

GOLDEN BOOT WINNER AND FIVE TIMES LEAGUE CHAMPION?

8 SIGNED TO **ARSENAL** FROM **SOUTHAMPTON** IN 2014, WHICH **ENGLAND** INTERNATIONAL DEFENDER WAS LOANED OUT TO **MIDDLESBROUGH** AND THEN VOTED **FULHAM'S** PLAYER OF THE SEASON WHILE ON LOAN TO **THE COTTAGERS?**

" ... AND THE TYNE."

THE SECOND MOST-CAPPED *ENGLAND* NATIONAL TEAM FULL-BACK, *KENNY SANSOM* MADE HIS NAME AT *CRYSTAL PALACE* AS THE TEAM ROSE FROM THE THIRD TIER TO THE TOP FLIGHT IN THE 1970S. IN HIS EIGHT SEASONS WITH *ARSENAL*, HE PLAYED 394 TIMES AND WON THE LEAGUE CUP, BUT BY THE TIME HE JOINED *NEWCASTLE UNITED* IN LATE 1988, HE HADN'T PLAYED A FIRST TEAM GAME IN FOUR MONTHS.

NAME THESE OTHER *GUNNERS* WITH GEORDIE LINKS:

1 FOLLOWING A SUCCESSFUL LOAN PERIOD, AN *ARSENAL* MIDFIELDER JOINED *NEWCASTLE* IN A £25 MILLION DEAL IN 2021.

2 *ENGLAND* CENTRAL DEFENDER WHO STARTED HIS CAREER WITH *TOTTENHAM HOTSPUR*, HAD TWO SPELLS AT *ARSENAL* AND ENDED HIS PLAYING DAYS AT *NEWCASTLE UNITED* IN 2011 BEFORE EVENTUALLY GOING INTO MANAGEMENT.

3 *ARSENAL* YOUNGSTER WHO WENT ON TO WIN THE PREMIER LEAGUE GOLDEN BOOT WITH *NEWCASTLE* IN 1994.

4 *ENGLAND* INTERNATIONAL INSIDE-FORWARD WHO WON TWO LEAGUE TITLES AND THE FA CUP WITH *THE GUNNERS* IN THE 1930S BEFORE JOINING SECOND TIER *NEWCASTLE UNITED* IN 1937.

5 CAPPED 27 TIMES BY *FRANCE*, RIGHT-BACK WHO JOINED *ARSENAL* IN 2014 AFTER A SEASON WITH *NEWCASTLE UNITED*.

6 *ENGLAND* CENTRE-FORWARD WHO WON THE GOLDEN BOOT WITH *NEWCASTLE UNITED* IN 1975 AND WITH *ARSENAL* IN 1977.

7 FORMER *BARNSLEY* CENTRAL DEFENDER WHO REACHED THE 1974 FA CUP FINAL WITH *NEWCASTLE UNITED* BEFORE SPENDING A SEASON WITH *THE GUNNERS*.

8 HIS 1960 TRANSFER TO *ARSENAL* FROM *NEWCASTLE* BECAME A LANDMARK LEGAL CASE IN PLAYERS' RIGHTS.

9 ***SCOTLAND*** MIDFIELDER WHOSE TWO LEG BREAKS DERAILED HIS ***ARSENAL*** CAREER IN THE MID-1970S. HE WON THE 1977 LEAGUE CUP WITH ***ASTON VILLA*** BEFORE SUFFERING ANOTHER LEG BREAK, AND LATER HAD A BRIEF LOAN SPELL WITH ***NEWCASTLE.***

10 FORMER ***NEWCASTLE UNITED*** FULL-BACK WHO COLLAPSED AND DIED, AT THE AGE OF 33, WHILE PLAYING FOR ***WOOLWICH ARSENAL*** DURING THE FIRST WORLD WAR, HE WAS BURIED IN HIS ***ARSENAL*** SHIRT.

THE BOYS OF 1979

HAVING PLAYED WITH **NEWRY TOWN** AND **SHAMROCK ROVERS**, **PAT JENNINGS** LEFT IRELAND AS A TEENAGER TO JOIN **WATFORD**. ONE EXCELLENT SEASON WITH THE THIRD DIVISION SIDE CONVINCED **TOTTENHAM HOTSPUR** TO SIGN HIM IN 1964. IN HIS 13 YEARS AT **WHITE HART LANE** HE WON THE FA CUP, TWO LEAGUE CUPS AND THE UEFA CUP. IN 1977, THINKING THAT THEY HAD ENJOYED HIS BEST YEARS, **SPURS** ALLOWED **JENNINGS** TO JOIN **ARSENAL**. THE BIG IRISHMAN PROVED THEM WRONG -- HE SPENT THE NEXT EIGHT YEARS AT **HIGHBURY**, HELPING **ARSENAL** TO FOUR CUP FINALS IN THREE SUCCESSIVE YEARS; THE FA CUP FINAL IN 1978, 1979, AND 1980, AS WELL AS THE EUROPEAN CUP WINNERS' CUP FINAL. HE RETURNED TO **SPURS** IN 1985, MAINLY TO TRAIN AND MAINTAIN FITNESS FOR **NORTHERN IRELAND'S** 1986 WORLD CUP CAMPAIGN. THE FIRST PLAYER IN ENGLISH FOOTBALL TO RACK UP 1,000 SENIOR APPEARANCES, HE WAS CAPPED 119 TIMES BY HIS COUNTRY.

HIS ONE TROPHY WITH **ARSENAL** WAS THE 1979 FA CUP. WHICH CLUBS DID THE FOLLOWING MEMBERS OF THAT TEAM JOIN FROM **ARSENAL?**

1   *PAT RICE*

2   *SAMMY NELSON*

3   *BRIAN TALBOT*

4   *DAVID O'LEARY*

5   *WILLIE YOUNG*

6   *LIAM BRADY*

7   *ALAN SUNDERLAND*

8 *FRANK STAPLETON*

9 *DAVID PRICE*

10 *GRAHAM RIX*

11 *STEVE WALFORD*

BAD BOYS! BAD BOYS!

DURING THE **ARSÈNE WENGER** AND **ALEX FERGUSON** ERA, RELATIONS BETWEEN **ARSENAL** AND **MANCHESTER UNITED** WERE FRACTIOUS AT BEST. IN 2004, WHEN A DISPUTED PENALTY SPARKED A 2-0 LOSS TO **UNITED** AND ENDED **ARSENAL'S** RECORD 49-GAME UNBEATEN STREAK, TEMPERS BOILED OVER IN THE TUNNEL AFTER THE GAME AND IN A BRAWL DUBBED *"THE BATTLE OF THE BUFFET"* BY THE TABLOIDS, A SLICE OF PIZZA WAS THROWN AT THE **UNITED** MANAGER -- ALLEGEDLY BY **CESC FÀBREGAS**. FOR HIS POST-GAME COMMENTS, IN WHICH HE LAMBASTED THE REFEREE AND CALLED **RUUD VAN NISTELROOY** A CHEAT, **WENGER** WAS FINED £15,000.

IDENTIFY THESE OTHER BAD BOY **GUNNERS:**

1 WHICH GOALKEEPER WAS FINED AND DROPPED FROM THE TEAM AFTER BEING CAUGHT SMOKING IN THE SHOWERS AFTER A LOSS TO **SOUTHAMPTON** IN 2015?

2 WHICH CENTRE-HALF WAS ONE OF THE *"COPENHAGEN FIVE"* GROUP OF PLAYERS BANNED FOR LIFE FOR PLAYING FOR **SCOTLAND** AFTER A BOOZY, BRAWLING NIGHT OUT IN THE DANISH CAPITAL IN 1975?

3 AFTER A KNEE INJURY ENDED HIS CAREER BEFORE HIS 21ST BIRTHDAY, WHICH STRIKER WAS STABBED SIX TIMES AND LOST 40 PINTS OF BLOOD WHEN A DRUG DEAL ON THE OLD KENT ROAD WENT WRONG IN 1985, RACKED UP CONVICTIONS FOR ROBBERIES AND WAS DEAD OF A HEROIN OVERDOSE BEFORE HIS 40TH BIRTHDAY?

4 WHICH BRAZILIAN'S PROPOSED £6 MILLION MOVE TO **ARSENAL** IN 2000 WAS THROWN INTO DOUBT WHEN HE WAS REFUSED ENTRY TO BRITAIN WITH A FORGED PASSPORT?

5 RELEASED FROM PRISON IN 2005 FOLLOWING A DRINK-DRIVING CONVICTION, WHICH **ARSENAL** WINGER, ON LOAN AT **BIRMINGHAM CITY**, PLAYED WITH AN ELECTRONIC ANKLE TAG?

6 WHICH STRIKER WAS BANNED AND FINED £80,000 BY UEFA FOR DISPLAYING UNDERPANTS ADVERTISING **PADDY POWER?**

7 WHICH ***ARSENAL*** HARDMAN'S LIFE OF CRIME INCLUDED CONVICTIONS FOR KEEPING A BROTHEL, CONSPIRACY TO COUNTERFEIT COINS AND TRYING TO SMUGGLE PORN INTO THE UK?

8 WHICH FORMER ***ARSENAL*** STAR'S VISIT TO A LOS ANGELES CLINIC FOR INTRAVENOUS VITAMIN TREATMENT BREACHED THE WORLD ANTI-DOPING AGENCY'S RULES AND LANDED HIM WITH A LENGTHY BAN?

9 WHICH ***ARSENAL*** CAPTAIN CRASHED HIS CAR INTO A WALL IN 1990 WHILE FOUR TIMES OVER THE LEGAL LIMIT, EARNING HIMSELF A STAY AT HER MAJESTY'S PLEASURE?

10 YEARS BEFORE FINDING SUCCESS AS AN ***ARSENAL*** AND ***ENGLAND*** STRIKER, NON-PAYMENT OF DRIVING FINES LANDED WHICH TEEN BEHIND BARS IN 1982?

STROLLER'S PACE

GEORGE GRAHAM WAS BORN IN BARGEDDIE, SCOTLAND, IN 1944, THE YOUNGEST OF SEVEN CHILDREN. HIS FATHER DIED OF TUBERCULOSIS WHEN GEORGE WAS BARELY A MONTH OLD AND THE FAMILY KNEW GREAT HARDSHIP. A TALENTED FOOTBALLER, GEORGE ATTRACTED THE INTEREST OF A NUMBER OF ENGLISH CLUBS AND SIGNED FOR ASTON VILLA AT THE AGE OF 15, TURNING PROFESSIONAL ON HIS 17TH BIRTHDAY IN 1961.

1 HE CHOSE ASTON VILLA TO LAUNCH HIS CAREER BECAUSE THE FAMILY LIKED THE MANAGER. CAN YOU NAME THAT MANAGER?

2 WHICH MANAGER SIGNED GEORGE TO CHELSEA IN 1964?

3 HE WON THE LEAGUE CUP WITH CHELSEA IN 1965 -- WHO WERE THE OPPONENTS?

4 HE JOINED ARSENAL IN 1966 AND WENT ON TO WIN THE INTER-CITIES FAIRS CUP AND A LEAGUE AND FA CUP DOUBLE. DURING THAT TIME, HE MADE HIS SCOTLAND DEBUT -- WHO WAS THE MANAGER WHO GAVE HIM HIS FIRST CAP IN OCTOBER, 1971?

5 WHO WAS THE MANAGER WHO SIGNED GEORGE TO MANCHESTER UNITED IN LATE 1972, JUST WEEKS BEFORE LOSING HIS JOB?

6 NAME ONE OF THE THREE CLUBS HE PLAYED FOR AFTER LEAVING UNITED -- TWO IN ENGLAND, ONE IN THE STATES.

7 HE EMBARKED ON HIS FIRST JOB IN MANAGEMENT WITH WHICH THIRD TIER CLUB IN 1982?

8 HE SPENT NINE YEARS WITH ARSENAL, STEERING THE CLUB TO MULTIPLE TROPHIES, INCLUDING TWO LEAGUE TITLES, THE FA CUP, TWO LEAGUE CUPS AND THE EUROPEAN CUP WINNERS' CUP. WHAT SCANDAL CAUSED GEORGE TO LOSE HIS JOB?

9 FOLLOWING A ONE-YEAR BAN, HE SUCCEEDED HOWARD WILKINSON AS MANAGER OF WHICH CLUB?

10 HIS FINAL JOB IN MANAGEMENT WAS WITH WHICH CLUB?

THE FRONT MAN

PAUL MARINER, THE *ENGLAND* CENTRE-FORWARD WHO SUCCUMBED TO BRAIN CANCER IN 2021 AT THE AGE OF 68, WAS A HUGE HEAVY METAL FAN. HIS POSTHUMOUS AUTOBIOGRAPHY -- *"MY ROCK AN ROLL FOOTBALL STORY"* -- FEATURES A FOREWORD WRITTEN BY HIS BEST FRIEND, *IAN GILLAN* OF *DEEP PURPLE* FAME.

1 HAVING PLAYED FOR LANCASHIRE SIDE *CHORLEY*, *MARINER* TURNED PRO WITH *PLYMOUTH ARGYLE* IN 1973. WHO WAS THE MANAGER, A FORMER *ENGLAND* AND *BLACKPOOL* GOALKEEPER, WHO SIGNED *MARINER* TO THE CLUB?

2 WHO WAS THE MANAGER WHO SIGNED *MARINER* TO *IPSWICH TOWN* FOR A CLUB RECORD £220,000 IN 1976?

3 WHO WAS THE MANAGER WHO GAVE *MARINER* HIS FIRST *ENGLAND* CAP IN MARCH, 1977?

4 HE WON THE FA CUP IN 1978 WHEN *IPSWICH TOWN* DEFEATED WHICH OPPONENTS 1-0?

5 *MARINER* SCORED ONCE AS *IPSWICH TOWN* RAN OUT 5-4 WINNERS ON AGGREGATE OVER WHICH DUTCH OPPONENTS TO WIN THE UEFA CUP IN 1981?

6 WHO WAS THE MANAGER WHO SIGNED HIM TO *ARSENAL* IN 1984?

7 AFTER TWO YEARS AT *HIGHBURY* HE JOINED *PORTSMOUTH*, WHERE HE PLAYED UNDER WHICH FORMER *ARSENAL* STAR?

8 AFTER PLAYING AND COACHING IN AUSTRALIA, THE STATES AND MALTA, HE BECAME ASSISTANT TO WHICH FORMER *LIVERPOOL* AND *SCOTLAND* DEFENDER AT THE *NEW ENGLAND REVOLUTION?*

9 HE WAS APPOINTED MANAGER OF *PLYMOUTH ARGYLE* IN LATE 2009 AND STEPPED DOWN IN 2010 WHEN HE WAS REPLACED BY WHICH FORMER *MANCHESTER CITY* AND *SUNDERLAND* BOSS?

10 HIS FINAL MANAGEMENT POST WAS WITH WHICH MLS TEAM?

"CELEBRATE GOOD TIMES ... COME ON!"

ONE OF THE MOST ICONIC GOAL CELEBRATIONS IN **ARSENAL** HISTORY FOLLOWED **CHARLIE GEORGE'S** EXTRA-TIME WINNER AGAINST **LIVERPOOL** IN THE 1971 FA CUP FINAL. WITH THE SCORE TIED AT 1-1, THE ISLINGTON MAVERICK SCORED WITH A LONG-RANGE WINNER AND HIT THE TURF, LYING ON HIS BACK WITH ARMS OUTSTRETCHED UNTIL HE WAS PICKED UP BY OTHER MEMBERS OF THE TEAM. THE GOAL WAS ENOUGH TO SECURE THE SECOND PART OF A FAMOUS LEAGUE AND FA CUP DOUBLE.

AFTER LEAVING **ARSENAL** FOR **DERBY COUNTY** IN 1978, **CHARLIE GEORGE** WENT ON TO PLAY FOR **SOUTHAMPTON** AND TEAMS IN THE UNITED STATES, HONG KONG AND SCOTLAND BEFORE RETIRING IN 1983.

WHICH CLUB DID THESE MEMBERS OF THE HISTORIC DOUBLE-WINNING SQUAD JOIN AFTER LEAVING **ARSENAL**? (**BOB WILSON** RETIRED WHEN HIS **ARSENAL** CAREER WAS OVER AND IS OMITTED FROM THE LIST.)

1 *PAT RICE*

2 *BOB MCNAB*

3 *PETER STOREY*

4 *FRANK MCLINTOCK*

5 *PETER SIMPSON*

6 *GEORGE ARMSTRONG*

7 *GEORGE GRAHAM*

8 *JOHN RADFORD*

9 *RAY KENNEDY*

10 *JOHN ROBERTS*

11 *JON SAMMELS*

"I'VE GOT THE MUSIC IN ME!"

HAVING SET A LEAGUE RECORD OF NOT CONCEDING A GOAL IN 903 COMPETITIVE MINUTES IN THE CZECH TOP FLIGHT WITH *SPARTA PRAGUE*, *PETR ČECH* SPENT TWO SEASONS WITH *RENNES* BEFORE JOINING *CHELSEA* IN 2004. IN HIS ELEVEN SEASONS AT THE CLUB HE WON AN IMPRESSIVE ARRAY OF HONOURS, INCLUDING THE UEFA CHAMPIONS LEAGUE, THE EUROPA LEAGUE AND FOUR PREMIER LEAGUE TITLES. HIS MOVE TO *ARSENAL* IN 2015 ELICITED DEATH THREATS FROM SOME DISGRUNTLED *CHELSEA* FANS!

ČECH IS AN ACCOMPLISHED DRUMMER WHO REGULARLY POSTS HIS MUSIC VIDEOS TO YOUTUBE. HE RECORDED A CHARITY SINGLE WITH *QUEEN'S ROGER TAYLOR* AND IN 2020, HE JOINED FOLK ROCK BAND *WILLS & THE WILLING*. IDENTIFY THESE OTHER *ARSENAL* LINKS TO MUSIC:

1 WHICH FORWARD ANNOUNCED HIS TRANSFER FROM *ARSENAL* TO *MANCHESTER UNITED* BY RELEASING A VIDEO OF HIM PLAYING *"GLORY, GLORY MAN UNITED"* ON THE PIANO?

2 WHICH *ARSENAL* STAR RELEASED A SINGLE, CO-WRITTEN AND PRODUCED BY ONE OF *THE PET SHOP BOYS*, THAT REACHED NUMBER 43 ON THE POP CHARTS IN 1993?

3 WHILE AT MANCHESTER UNITED IN 1999, WHICH FORMER *ARSENAL* STRIKER RELEASED THE SINGLE *"OUTSTANDING"*?

4 WHICH TV PUNDIT AND PRESENTER, A FORMER FOOTBALL STAR HIMSELF, ADAPTED *"RULE BRITANNIA"* TO *"GOOD OLD ARSENAL"* AND CREATED A SINGLE THAT SPENT 16 WEEKS ON THE POP CHARTS IN 1971?

5 *ARSENAL'S* 1998 FA CUP FINAL SINGLE -- WHICH REACHED NUMBER NINE ON THE CHARTS -- WAS A REWORKING OF WHICH CLASSIC *DONNA SUMMER* POP SONG?

6 WHICH DUTCH FORWARD, WHO WAS CAPPED 17 TIMES BY *GHANA* AND PLAYED FOR *ARSENAL, BIRMINGHAM CITY, CARDIFF CITY, PORTSMOUTH* AND CLUBS IN GREECE, QATAR, PORTUGAL AND THE NETHERLANDS, WAS A MEMBER OF AMSTERDAM RAP GROUP *DE FELLAS* AND RECORDS UNDER THE STAGE NAME *BLOW?*

"LIFE IS SO GOOD IN AMERICA ..."

WINNER OF TWO PREMIER LEAGUES AND THREE FA CUPS WITH **ARSENAL**, **SWEDEN** INTERNATIONAL **FREDDIE LJUNGBERG** REPRESENTED HIS COUNTRY AT FIVE MAJOR TOURNAMENTS AND PLAYED WITH CLUBS IN SWEDEN, SCOTLAND, THE UNITED STATES, JAPAN AND INDIA.

LJUNGBERG PLAYED FOR **SEATTLE SOUNDERS** AND **CHICAGO FIRE**. NAME THESE OTHER **ARSENAL** STARS WHO PLAYED IN NORTH AMERICA:

1 A LONDONER CAPPED FIVE TIMES BY THE **REPUBLIC OF IRELAND**, HE PLAYED WITH **WATFORD**, **LEYTON ORIENT** AND **QPR**, SPENT TWO SEASONS WITH **ARSENAL** AND A SEASON AT **ALDERSHOT** BEFORE SIGNING FOR THE **LOS ANGELES AZTECS** IN 1977.

2 FRENCH FULL-BACK WHO WON CUP HONOURS WITH **ARSENAL** AND **MANCHESTER CITY** BEFORE SPENDING SIX MONTHS IN ITALY WITH **BENEVENTO** AND THEN JOINING MLS TEAM **MONTREAL IMPACT** IN 2018.

3 AFTER WINNING THREE FA CUPS IN HIS 12 SEASONS WITH **ARSENAL**, HE FOLLOWED A LOAN SPELL WITH **NORWICH CITY** WITH FOUR SEASONS AT **WEST BROMWICH ALBION** -- DURING WHICH TIME HE EXPERIENCED RELEGATION AND PROMOTION -- BEFORE SIGNING FOR **INTER MIAMI**.

4 FORMER **MANCHESTER UNITED**, **ARSENAL**, **MANCHESTER CITY**, **EVERTON** AND **BOLTON WANDERERS** FORWARD WHO PLAYED IN THE STATES FOR **ATLANTA CHIEFS**, **FORT LAUDERDALE STRIKERS** AND **MINNESOTA STRIKERS** IN THE 1980S, BEFORE EMBARKING ON A STELLAR COACHING CAREER.

5 **NORTHERN IRELAND** INTERNATIONAL WHO SCORED **ARSENAL'S** WINNER IN THE 1993 LEAGUE CUP FINAL, HE PLAYED FOR **DALLAS BURN** AND LATER MANAGED **FC DALLAS**.

6 **ARSENAL'S** 1971 FA CUP FINAL HERO WHO JOINED THE **MINNESOTA KICKS** FROM **DERBY COUNTY** IN 1978.

7 A CHAMPIONS LEAGUE, FA CUP AND QUADRUPLE PREMIER LEAGUE WINNER WITH **MANCHESTER UNITED**, A FRENCH FULL-BACK WHO LEFT **ARSENAL** FOR **WERDER BREMEN** AND THEN JOINED THE **PORTLAND TIMBERS** IN 2013.

8 MULTIPLE LEAGUE AND FA CUP WINNER WITH **ARSENAL**, A PREMIER LEAGUE, CHAMPIONS LEAGUE AND EUROPA LEAGUE WINNER WITH **CHELSEA**, AN ENGLAND INTERNATIONAL WHO SPENT THREE SEASONS IN THE MLS WITH **LOS ANGELES GALAXY**.

9 A WORLD CUP WINNER WHO JOINED **ARSENAL** FROM **EVERTON**, PLAYED WITH **PHILADELPHIA FURY** AND THE **VANCOUVER WHITECAPS** AND LATER MANAGED A NUMBER OF ENGLISH CLUBS.

10 **ARSENAL** AND **BARCELONA** GOALSCORING LEGEND WHO WON THE 2013 MLS SUPPORTERS SHIELD WITH **NEW YORK RED BULLS**.

SUPERMAC

WHEN **ARSENAL** SIGNED THE PROLIFIC **MALCOLM MACDONALD** FROM **NEWCASTLE UNITED** IN 1976, THE AGREED FEE WAS *"ONE THIRD OF A MILLION POUNDS".* A CHEQUE IN THE AMOUNT OF £333,333.33 WAS DULY PREPARED FOR THE **ARSENAL** CHAIRMAN TO SIGN ... BUT HE INSISTED THAT THE AMOUNT BE AMENDED TO £333,333.34 TO AVOID ANY POSSIBILITY OF THE DEAL BEING DERAILED OVER A MINOR QUIBBLE!

1 AFTER LAUNCHING HIS CAREER AT NON-LEAGUE **TONBRIDGE ANGELS**, TEENAGER **MACDONALD** WAS SIGNED TO **FULHAM**, THE CLUB HE SUPPORTED AS A BOY, IN 1968 BY WHICH MANAGER?

2 HE JOINED WHICH THIRD-TIER CLUB, MANAGED AT THAT TIME BY **ALEC STOCK**, IN 1969?

3 TWO YEARS LATER, HE WAS SOLD TO **NEWCASTLE UNITED** FOR £175,000, ARRIVING AT **ST JAMES' PARK** IN A ROLLS ROYCE! WHO WAS THE MANAGER, A **NEWCASTLE UNITED** LEGEND AS A PLAYER, WHO SIGNED HIM?

4 HE MADE HIS **ENGLAND** DEBUT IN 1972 -- AGAINST WHICH COUNTRY DID HE SCORE FIVE GOALS IN ONE GAME IN 1975?

5 WHO WAS THE MANAGER WHO SIGNED HIM TO **ARSENAL** IN 1976?

6 HE WON THE GOLDEN BOOT IN HIS DEBUT SEASON, THE FIRST TIME AN **ARSENAL** PLAYER HAD FINISHED TOP LEAGUE SCORER SINCE WHICH PLAYER IN THE 1947-48 SEASON?

7 IN 1978, HE SUFFERED THE KNEE INJURY THAT EFFECTIVELY ENDED HIS CAREER, ALTHOUGH HE DID PLAY FOR A COUPLE OF MONTHS IN 1979 WITH WHICH SWEDISH TEAM?

8 AFTER RETIRING FROM PLAYING, HE MOVED INTO MANAGEMENT, STEERING WHICH CLUB TO A PROMOTION IN 1982?

9 HIS SECOND, AND FINAL, JOB IN MANAGEMENT WAS WITH WHICH YORKSHIRE CLUB?

PADDY POWERFUL!

PATRICK VIEIRA WAS BORN IN SENEGAL BUT MOVED TO FRANCE WITH HIS FAMILY WHEN HE WAS EIGHT YEARS OLD. BECAUSE HIS GRANDFATHER SERVED IN THE FRENCH ARMY, **PATRICK** WAS ELIGIBLE FOR FRENCH NATIONALITY. HE WENT ON TO WIN THE 1998 WORLD CUP AND EURO 2000 WITH **FRANCE**. IN ACKNOWLEDGEMENT OF THE WORLD CUP WIN, THE **FRANCE** SQUAD WERE ALL AWARDED THE COUNTRY'S HIGHEST ORDER OF MERIT AND MADE KNIGHTS OF THE LEGION OF HONOUR.

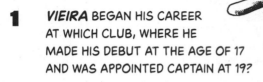

1   **VIEIRA** BEGAN HIS CAREER AT WHICH CLUB, WHERE HE MADE HIS DEBUT AT THE AGE OF 17 AND WAS APPOINTED CAPTAIN AT 19?

2   HE JOINED **AC MILAN** IN 1995, WHERE HE PLAYED ALONGSIDE WHICH FRENCH DEFENDER WHO WOULD ALSO WIN WORLD CUP AND EURO HONOURS ALONGSIDE HIM IN THE **FRANCE** TEAM?

3   HE JOINED **ARSENAL** IN AUGUST, 1996, SIGNING ON THE SAME DAY AS WHICH FELLOW FRENCH PLAYER, WHO WOULD LATER MANAGE **LYON** AND **ASTON VILLA?**

4   **VIEIRA** SPENT NINE SEASONS WITH **THE GUNNERS**, BETWEEN 1996 AND 2005 -- HOW MANY PREMIER LEAGUE TITLES DID HE WIN?

5   HE SIGNED FOR **JUVENTUS** IN 2005, WHERE HE WAS REUNITED WITH WHICH FUTURE **ENGLAND** MANAGER, WHO HAD SIGNED HIM TO **AC MILAN** AS A TEENAGER?

6   JOINING **INTERNAZIONALE** IN 2006, HE PLAYED UNDER WHICH TWO MANAGERS WHO WOULD LATER WIN PREMIER LEAGUE TITLES?

7   AFTER WINNING THREE SERIE A TITLES IN THREE-AND-A-HALF SEASONS WITH **INTER**, HE JOINED **MANCHESTER CITY** IN JANUARY, 2010. WHO WAS THE MANAGER WHO SIGNED HIM?

8 HE WON THE FA CUP WITH *MANCHESTER CITY* WHEN THEY DEFEATED WHICH TEAM IN THE 2011 FINAL?

9 AFTER RETIRING, HE MANAGED *CITY'S ELITE DEVELOPMENT SQUAD* BEFORE ACCEPTING THE MANAGER POST WITH WHICH TEAM IN 2016?

10 IN 2018, *VIEIRA* WAS APPOINTED MANAGER OF WHICH FRENCH TEAM?

11 IN 2021, *VIEIRA* SUCCEEDED WHICH MANAGER AS BOSS OF *CRYSTAL PALACE?*

LUCKY NUMBER 9?

THE NUMBER 9 IS THOUGHT TO BE LUCKY IN MANY CULTURES. WHEN **PARK CHU-YOUNG** JOINED **ARSENAL** IN 2011, THE SOUTH KOREAN WAS ALLOCATED THE COVETED NO. 9 SHIRT ... BUT IT PROVED TO BE ANYTHING BUT LUCKY FOR HIM. IT WAS SOON EVIDENT THAT HE WAS LOST IN ENGLISH FOOTBALL AND HE PLUMMETED DOWN THE PECKING ORDER SO QUICKLY THAT, WITHIN A YEAR, HE WAS FARMED OUT ON LOAN TO **CELTA VIGO** AND HIS SQUAD NUMBER GIVEN TO THE INCOMING **LUKAS PODOLSKI**.

NAME THESE OTHER WEARERS OF THE **ARSENAL** NO. 9 SHIRT:

1 IN 2017, WHICH SPANISH STRIKER, WHO WOULD LATER PLAY FOR **WEST HAM UNITED**, HAD HIS NO. 9 SHIRT TAKEN BY THE INCOMING **ALEXANDRE LACAZETTE** AND WAS THEN SHIPPED OUT ON LOAN TO HIS PREVIOUS CLUB, **DEPORTIVO LA CORUÑA?**

2 JUST MONTHS AFTER HIS 2007 TRANSFER FROM **DINAMO ZAGREB**, WHICH **CROATIA** INTERNATIONAL SUFFERED A TERRIBLE LEG BREAK AND ANKLE DISLOCATION ?

3 NICKNAMED **"LA BESTIA"** -- **"THE BEAST"** -- WHICH POWERFUL BRAZILIAN WAS ON FIRE AT **SEVILLA**, SPLUTTERED AT **REAL MADRID** AND, OTHER THAN THE FOUR GOALS HE NETTED AGAINST **LIVERPOOL** IN THE LEAGUE CUP IN EARLY 2007, BARELY FLICKERED AT **ARSENAL?**

4 WHO ARRIVED AT **ARSENAL** FROM **EVERTON** IN 2001 AS A LAUDED, £8 MILLION GOAL-POACHER AND DUE TO INJURIES AND POOR FORM, SOON BECAME A BENCH-WARMER AND WAS BACK AT **EVERTON** ON LOAN BY 2003?

5 WHICH WORLD CUP GOLDEN BOOT-WINNER ARRIVED AT **ARSENAL** FROM **REAL MADRID** IN 1999, AND LASTED JUST ONE SEASON BEFORE MOVING ON TO **WEST HAM UNITED?**

MONEY MATTERS

HAVING IMPRESSED AT EURO 2008, **ANDREY ARSHAVIN** WAS RECRUITED BY **THE GUNNERS** IN THE 2008-09 WINTER WINDOW. HIS £15 MILLION TRANSFER FROM **ZENIT SAINT PETERSBURG** MADE HIM THE MOST EXPENSIVE PLAYER IN **ARSENAL'S** HISTORY TO THAT POINT.

CAN YOU IDENTIFY THESE BIG MONEY **ARSENAL** ACQUISITIONS?

1   1958: **PRESTON NORTH END** -- £21,000

2   1959: **SWANSEA TOWN** -- £42,750

3   1960: **NEWCASTLE UNITED** -- £47,500

4   1962: **TORINO** -- £70,000

5   1964: **LEICESTER CITY** -- £80,000

6   1968: **COVENTRY CITY** -- £90,000

7   1970: **HIBERNIAN** -- £100,000

8   1958: **EVERTON** -- £220,000

9   1979: **IPSWICH TOWN** -- £450,000

10   1980: **CRYSTAL PALACE** -- £1,250,000

11   1991: **CRYSTAL PALACE** -- £2,500,000

12   1995: **INTERNAZIONALE**-- £7,500,000

13   1999: **JUVENTUS** -- £11,000,000

14   2000: **BORDEAUX** -- £13,000,000

15   2018: **SAMPDORIA** -- £26,000,000

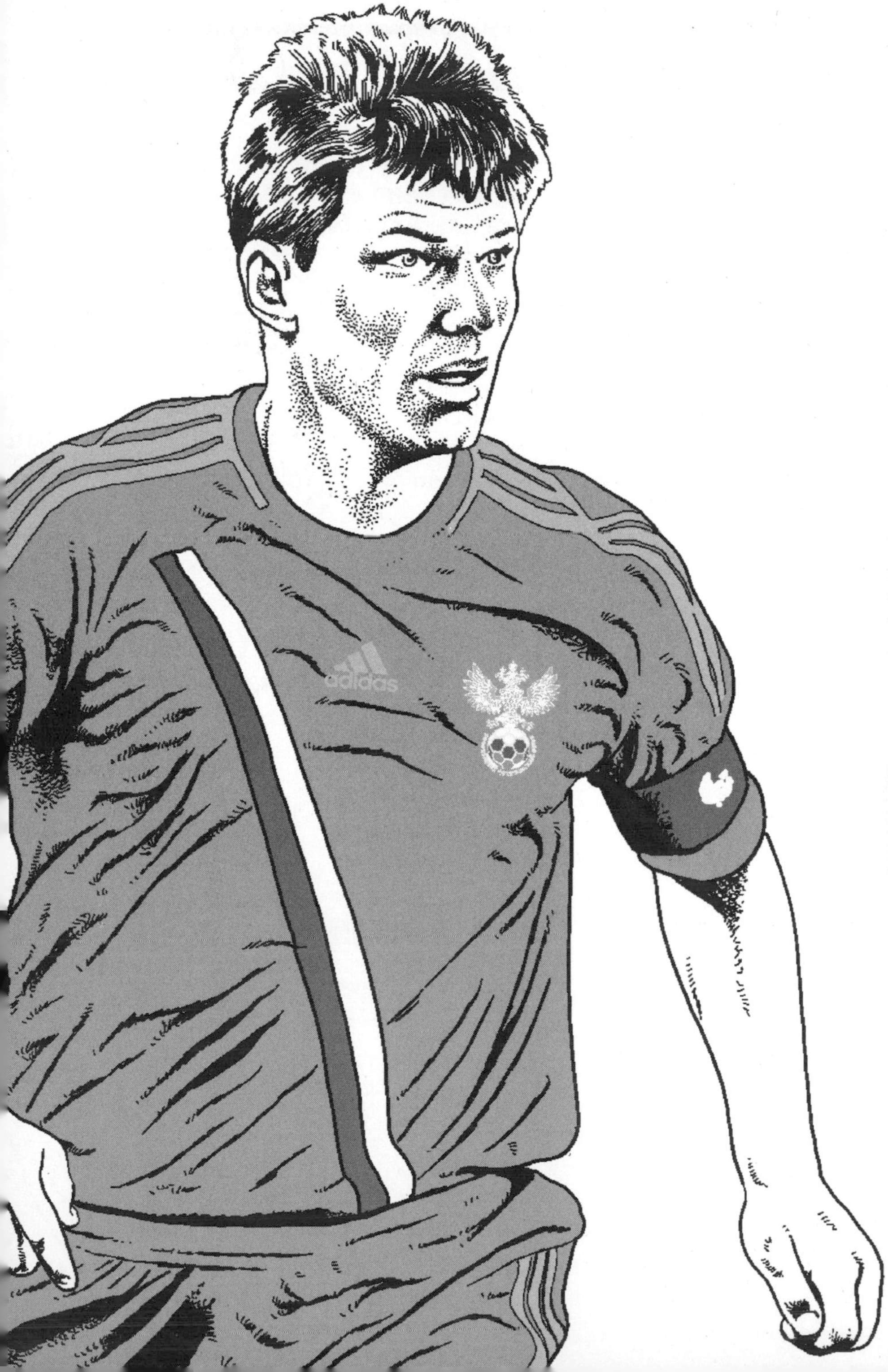
adidas

LAND OF THE RISING SUN

LUKAS PODOLSKI WAS BORN IN GILWICE, POLAND, ON JUNE 4, 1985, BUT RAISED IN GERMANY FROM THE AGE OF TWO. HE WON PROMOTION TO THE TOP FLIGHT WITH **FC KÖLN**, A LEAGUE AND CUP DOUBLE WITH **BAYERN MUNICH**, THE FA CUP WITH **ARSENAL** AND TURKISH CUP AND SUPERCUP HONOURS WITH **GALATASARAY**. A THREE-YEAR SPELL IN JAPAN WITH **VISSEL KOBE** BROUGHT AN EMPEROR'S CUP VICTORY. **PODOLSKI**, A WORLD CUP WINNER WITH **GERMANY** IN 2014, WHOSE OTHER CLUBS INCLUDE **INTERNAZIONALE** AND **ANTALYASPOR**, SIGNED FOR POLAND'S **GÓRNIK ZABRZE** IN 2021.

1 WHICH *BELGIUM* CENTRE-BACK, WHO WON HONOURS WITH *AJAX*, *ARSENAL* AND *BARCELONA*, JOINED *VISSEL KOBE* AND WON AN EMPEROR'S CUP IN 2019 AND JAPANESE SUPER CUP IN 2020?

2 WHICH JAPANESE WINGER JOINED *ARSENAL* IN 2011 AND WAS LOANED OUT TO A NUMBER OF CLUBS, INCLUDING *FEYENOORD*, *BOLTON WANDERERS*, *WIGAN ATHLETIC* AND *TWENTE* BEFORE SIGNING FOR *FC ST PAULI* IN 2015? HE RETURNED HOME FROM GERMANY IN 2021 TO JOIN *YOKOHAMA F. MARINOS*.

3 WHICH ARSENAL ACADEMY GRADUATE PLAYED FOR *BLACKBURN ROVERS*, *CHARLTON ATHLETIC*, *WOLVES*, *STOKE CITY*, *CARDIFF CITY*, *QPR* AND *SHEFFIELD WEDNESDAY*, PLAYED IN ITALY AND THAILAND AND JOINED *HOKKAIDO CONSADOLE SAPPORO* IN 2017 AFTER A SEASON WITH *JÚBILO IWATA?*

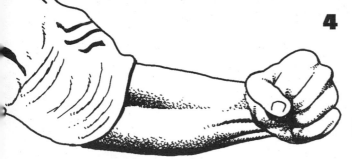

4 BEFORE TAKING THE *ARSENAL* JOB, *ARSÈNE WENGER* MANAGED WHICH JAPANESE TEAM?

5 DESPITE HAVING REPRESENTED *JAPAN* AT INTERNATIONAL LEVEL, WHICH FORWARD WAS DENIED A WORK PERMIT WHEN HE SIGNED TO *ARSENAL* IN 2016, AND HAS SINCE PLAYED WITH *VFB STUTTGART*, *HANNOVER 96* AND *PARTIZAN*, BEFORE JOINING *VFL BOCHUM* IN 2021?

6 CAPPED 82 TIMES BY *JAPAN*, WHICH MIDFIELDER HAD SPELLS ON LOAN WITH *ARSENAL* AND *FULHAM* FROM *GAMBA OSAKA*, SIGNED FOR *WEST BROMWICH ALBION*, PLAYED ON LOAN AT *CARDIFF CITY*, MOVED ON TO *GALATASARAY*, *EINTRACHT FRANKFURT*, AND *STADE RENNES* BEFORE HEADING BACK TO JAPANESE LEAGUE FOOTBALL IN 2010?

7 WHICH SWEDISH STAR, WHOSE CLUBS INCLUDE *ARSENAL*, *WEST HAM UNITED* AND *CELTIC*, JOINED *SHIMIZU S-PULSE* IN 2011?

OH, DANNY BOY

DANNY WELBECK MADE HIS **MANCHESTER UNITED** DEBUT AT THE AGE OF 17 AND HIS **ENGLAND** DEBUT AT THE AGE OF 20. HE MADE 42 APPEARANCES FOR HIS COUNTRY, SCORING 16 GOALS. THE ONLY **ARSENAL** PLAYERS TO SCORE MORE GOALS FOR **ENGLAND** DURING THEIR CAREERS ARE **DAVID PLATT** AND **TONY WOODCOCK**.

1   **WELBECK** PLAYED FOR **MANCHESTER UNITED** IN THE 2009 LEAGUE CUP FINAL -- WHO DID THEY BEAT ON PENALTIES TO WIN?

2   IN 2010, **DARREN FERGUSON** -- SON OF **UNITED** BOSS **SIR ALEX FERGUSON** -- TOOK **WELBECK** ON LOAN TO WHICH CLUB?

3   WHICH FORMER **MANCHESTER UNITED** PLAYER TOOK HIM ON LOAN AT **SUNDERLAND** IN THE 2010-11 SEASON?

4   WHO WAS THE **UNITED** MANAGER WHO SANCTIONED **WELBECK'S** TRANSFER TO **ARSENAL** IN 2014?

5   HE SCORED THE FIRST HAT-TRICK OF HIS SENIOR CAREER IN **ARSENAL'S** 4-1 UEFA CHAMPIONS LEAGUE WIN OVER WHICH TEAM IN OCTOBER, 2014?

6   HE WON THE FA CUP WITH **ARSENAL** IN 2017 -- WHO WERE THE OPPONENTS IN THE FINAL?

7   AFTER FIVE INJURY-PLAGUED SEASONS WITH **THE GUNNERS**, HE WAS TRANSFERRED TO **WATFORD** IN 2019. WHO WAS THE **ARSENAL** MANAGER WHO SANCTIONED THE MOVE?

8 **WELBECK** WAS WITH **WATFORD** FROM AUGUST 7, 2019 TO OCTOBER 6, 2020. INCREDIBLY, THE CLUB WENT THROUGH FIVE MANAGERS IN THAT PERIOD! HOW MANY OF THAT QUINTET CAN YOU NAME?

9 **WELBECK** SIGNED FOR **BRIGHTON & HOVE ALBION** -- AND WHICH MANAGER -- IN OCTOBER, 2019?

10 NAME THE FOUR **ENGLAND** MANAGERS UNDER WHOM **DANNY WELBECK** PLAYED BETWEEN HIS FIRST CAP ON MARCH 29, 2011 AND HIS 42ND APPEARANCE ON SEPTEMBER 11, 2018.

TOFFEE NOSED

THEO WALCOTT, THE BOY WONDER CAPTURED FROM **SOUTHAMPTON**, WHO WENT TO A WORLD CUP WITH **ENGLAND** BEFORE HE HAD EVEN MADE HIS LEAGUE DEBUT FOR **ARSENAL**, WON TWO FA CUPS IN HIS 13 SEASONS AS A **GUNNER**. HE SIGNED FOR **EVERTON** IN EARLY 2018, BEFORE REJOINING **SOUTHAMPTON** IN 2020.

NAME THESE OTHER **GUNNERS** WHO'VE PLAYED FOR **"THE TOFFEES"**.

1   NIGERIA WINGER WHO WON THE FA CUP WITH **ARSENAL** BEFORE JOINING **EVERTON** IN A £28 MILLION DEAL IN 2019.

2   WINGER CAPPED 58 TIMES BY **SWEDEN**, HE WON ALL THREE DOMESTIC TROPHIES WITH **ARSENAL** IN THE EARLY 1990S AND THE 1995 FA CUP WITH **EVERTON**.

3 LEAGUE TITLE WINNER WITH **EVERTON** AND THEN **ARSENAL** EITHER SIDE OF THE SECOND WORLD WAR, HE LATER MANAGED **MANCHESTER CITY** TO THE TITLE IN 1968 AND WAS ENGLAND CARETAKER MANAGER IN 1974.

4 **EVERTON'S** *"FOX IN THE BOX"*, HIS GOALSCORING EXPLOITS CONVINCED **ARSENAL** TO SIGN THE 20-YEAR-OLD IN 2001. THE MOVE DIDN'T PAN OUT AND HE WAS LOANED BACK TO *"THE TOFFEES"* IN 2003.

5 GOALKEEPER CAPPED TWICE BY **ENGLAND**, HE HAD THREE SPELLS WITH **IPSWICH TOWN**, PLAYED FOR **ARSENAL** AND **EVERTON** AND FINISHED HIS CAREER AT **MANCHESTER CITY**, JOINING THE COACHING STAFF WHEN HE RETIRED IN 2016.

6 A EUROPEAN CUP WINNER WITH **MANCHESTER UNITED** AT THE AGE OF 18 IN 1968.

SOUTH AFRICA

SCOTLAND CENTRE-HALF *FRANK MCLINTOCK* PLAYED ON THE LOSING SIDE IN TWO FA CUP FINALS WITH *LEICESTER CITY* BEFORE SIGNING FOR *THE GUNNERS* IN 1964 FOR A CLUB RECORD £80,000. *ARSENAL* PLAYER OF THE YEAR IN 1968, HE WON A LEAGUE AND FA CUP DOUBLE IN 1971, THE SEASON HE WAS VOTED FWA FOOTBALLER OF THE YEAR.

MCLINTOCK WAS ONE OF A NUMBER OF FOOTBALLERS, INCLUDING *BOBBY CHARLTON, BOBBY MOORE* AND *KEVIN KEEGAN*, WHO PLAYED IN SOUTH AFRICA IN THE 1970S. *MCLINTOCK* PLAYED FOR *CAPE TOWN CITY*, A TEAM THAT BOASTED *MICK CHANNON, FRANCIS LEE* AND *GEOFF HURST* IN ITS RANKS.

IDENTIFY THESE OTHERS WHO PLAYED IN SOUTH AFRICA:

1 *PORTUGAL* INTERNATIONAL WHO WON THE PREMIER LEAGUE WITH *ARSENAL* IN 1998, THE FIRST DIVISION WITH *FULHAM* IN 2001, PLAYED FOR *SOUTHAMPTON* AND *WEST HAM UNITED* AND HAD A BRIEF SPELL WITH THE *ORLANDO PIRATES* IN 2012.

2 INSIDE-FORWARD WHO JOINED *ARSENAL* FROM *NEWCASTLE UNITED* IN CONTROVERSIAL CIRCUMSTANCES, WON THE LEAGUE CUP IN 1972 WITH *STOKE CITY* AND LATER PLAYED FOR *CAPE TOWN CITY* AND *HELLENIC* IN SOUTH AFRICA.

3 FORMER *YORK CITY, NOTTINGHAM FOREST, ARSENAL* AND *SHEFFIELD UNITED* FORWARD WHOSE MANAGEMENT CAREER SAW HIM TAKE CHARGE OF A GREAT NUMBER OF TEAMS, INCLUDING *DURBAN CITY* IN SOUTH AFRICA, *ATLÉTICO MADRID* IN SPAIN, *DERBY COUNTY, SWANSEA CITY* AND TEAMS IN KUWAIT AND QATAR.

4 LONDON-BORN, *REPUBLIC OF IRELAND* CENTRE-HALF WHO PLAYED FOR *PORT ELIZABETH CITY* EARLY IN HIS CAREER, MOVED ON TO *LEYTON ORIENT, QUEENS PARK RANGERS, ARSENAL, ALDERSHOT, LOS ANGELES AZTECS* AND ENDED HIS CARER AT *BARNET* IN 1978.

GOALS! GOALS! GOALS!

ARSENAL'S ALL-TIME LEADING SCORER WITH 228 GOALS IN ALL COMPETITIONS, **THIERRY HENRY** WON THE PREMIER LEAGUE GOLDEN BOOT A RECORD FOUR TIMES, WON TWO FA CUPS AND TWO PREMIER LEAGUE TITLES WITH THE CLUB, INCLUDING ONE DURING AN UNBEATEN SEASON WITH THE TEAM DUBBED *"THE INVINCIBLES".*

IDENTIFY THESE OTHER PROLIFIC **ARSENAL** GOALSCORERS:

1   *185 GOALS:* 1991-1998

2   *178 GOALS:* 1929-1947

3   *149 GOALS:* 1964-1976

4   *139 GOALS:* 1923-1931

5   *139 GOALS:* 1934-1945

6   *137 GOALS:* 1948-1956

7   *132 GOALS:* 2004-2012

8   *125 GOALS:* 1926-1938

9   *124 GOALS:* 1928-1934

BALL OF FIRE!

THE YOUNGEST MEMBER OF **ENGLAND'S** 1966 WORLD CUP-WINNING TEAM, **ALAN BALL** PLAYED FOR AND MANAGED CLUBS IN ENGLAND, THE UNITED STATES, CANADA, SOUTH AFRICA, AUSTRALIA AND HONG KONG. HE DIED OF A HEART ATTACK IN 2007, AT THE AGE OF 61. HE WAS THE SECOND MEMBER OF THE 1966 WORLD CUP TEAM TO DIE, FOLLOWING **BOBBY MOORE** IN 1993.

1 AGED 17 YEARS AND 98 DAYS, **BALL** BECAME THE YOUNGEST DEBUTANT FOR WHICH LANCASHIRE CLUB?

2 FOLLOWING THE 1966 WORLD CUP TRIUMPH, HE JOINED **EVERTON** IN A RECORD BRITISH TRANSFER OF £112,000. WHO WAS THE LONG-SERVING MANAGER WHO SIGNED HIM TO **THE TOFFEES?**

3 HE WON A LEAGUE TITLE WITH **EVERTON** TWO YEARS AFTER PLAYING IN THE 1968 FA CUP FINAL LOSS TO WHICH TEAM?

4 HE SPENT FIVE YEARS WITH **THE GUNNERS** BUT THE CLOSEST HE CAME TO A TROPHY WAS WHEN HOLDERS **ARSENAL** LOST THE 1972 FA CUP FINAL TO WHICH TEAM?

5 MOVING ON TO **SOUTHAMPTON**, HE HELPED **THE SAINTS** RETURN TO THE TOP FLIGHT AND REACH A LEAGUE CUP FINAL. WHO WAS THE MANAGER WHO TOOK HIM TO **THE DELL?**

6 AFTER PLAYING FOR CLUBS IN ENGLAND, THE STATES, AUSTRALIA AND HONG KONG, EITHER AS PLAYER OR PLAYER/MANAGER, HE ENDED HIS PLAYING CAREER IN 1983 WITH WHICH TEAM WHOSE NICKNAME IS **THE PIRATES?**

7 HE SUCCEEDED **BOBBY CAMPBELL** AS MANAGER OF WHICH CLUB IN 1984, STEERING THEM TO PROMOTION AND RELEGATION DURING HIS FIVE-YEAR TENURE? (HE WOULD RETURN TO THE CLUB IN 1998 IN WHAT WOULD PROVE TO BE HIS FINAL POST IN MANAGEMENT).

8 WHILE MANAGING **EXETER CITY** IN 1992, HE ALSO WORKED AS AN **ENGLAND** COACH UNDER WHICH MANAGER?

9 IN 1994 AND 1995, HE COACHED THE LIKES OF **MATT LE TISSIER** AND **BRUCE GROBBELAAR** AS MANAGER OF WHICH CLUB?

10 IN HIS PENULTIMATE JOB IN MANAGEMENT, HE SUCCEEDED **BRIAN HORTON** AS MANAGER OF WHICH CLUB?

EXIT THE OX!

SON OF **STOKE CITY, PORTSMOUTH** AND **ENGLAND** STAR **MARK CHAMBERLAIN, ALEX OXLADE-CHAMBERLAIN** MADE HIS SENIOR DEBUT FOR **SOUTHAMPTON** AT THE AGE OF 16 YEARS AND 199 DAYS. HE JOINED **ARSENAL** A WEEK BEFORE HIS 18TH BIRTHDAY. IN HIS SEVEN SEASONS WITH **THE GUNNERS** HE WON THREE FA CUPS AND BECAME AN **ENGLAND** REGULAR, BEFORE SIGNING FOR **LIVERPOOL** IN 2017, HIS TRANSFER FEE OF £35 MILLION THE LARGEST **ARSENAL** HAVE RECEIVED.

TO WHICH TEAMS WERE THE FOLLOWING TRANSFERRED FROM **ARSENAL?**

1 **MARC OVERMARS** -- 2000

2 **SERGE GNABRY** -- 2016

3 **GILBERTO SILVA** -- 2008

4 **CARLOS VELA** -- 2007

5 **STEFAN SCHWARZ** -- 1995

6 **CHARLIE NICHOLAS** -- 1987

7 **EMMANUEL PETIT** -- 2000

8 **FRANCIS JEFFERS** -- 2004

9 **ALEX IWOBI** -- 2019

10 **JOHAN DJOUROU** -- 2014

11 **SANTI CAZORLA** -- 2018

12 **FRANCIS COQUELIN** -- 2017

13 **GERVINHO** -- 2013

14 **BRIAN MARWOOD** -- 1990

HALL OF FAMERS

SINCE 2002, THE ENGLISH FOOTBALL HALL OF FAME -- WHICH IS HOUSED AT THE NATIONAL FOOTBALL MUSEUM IN MANCHESTER -- HAS CELEBRATED SIGNIFICANT FIGURES IN THE ENGLISH GAME. *DAVID SEAMAN* IS ONE OF THREE *ARSENAL* GOALKEEPERS, ALONG WITH *PAT JENNINGS* AND *BOB WILSON*, WHO HAVE BEEN INDUCTED. IDENTIFY THESE OTHER *ARSENAL* PLAYERS INDUCTED INTO THE MEN'S SECTION:

1 2003: MIDFIELDER 1962-1983 -- *BLACKPOOL, EVERTON, ARSENAL, SOUTHAMPTON, BRISTOL ROVERS*

2 2003: FORWARD 1936-1955 -- *BURNLEY, EVERTON, CHELSEA, NOTTS COUNTY, BRENTFORD, ARSENAL*

3 2004: DEFENDER 1983-2002 -- *ARSENAL* (ENGLISH PLAYER)

4 2004: DEFENDER 1974-1995 -- *NOTTINGHAM FOREST, ARSENAL, MANCHESTER UNITED, SHEFFIELD WEDNESDAY, BARNSLEY, MIDDLESBROUGH*

5 2005: FORWARD 1925-1937 -- *PRESTON NORTH END, ARSENAL*

6 2005: FORWARD 1985-2000 -- *CRYSTAL PALACE, ARSENAL, WEST HAM UNITED, NOTTINGHAM FOREST, BURNLEY*

7 2006: MIDFIELDER 1973-1990 -- *ARSENAL, WEST HAM UNITED*

8 2007: FORWARD 1995-2006 -- *ARSENAL* (DUTCH PLAYER)

9 2008: FORWARD 1999-2012 -- *ARSENAL* (FRENCH PLAYER)

10 2009: MIDFIELDER 1928-1947 -- *EXETER CITY, ARSENAL*

11 2009: DEFENDER 1956-1977 -- *LEICESTER CITY, ARSENAL, QUEENS PARK RANGERS*

12 2010: FORWARD 1911-1928 -- *SUNDERLAND, ARSENAL*

13 2014: MIDFIELDER 1996-2011 -- *ARSENAL, MANCHESTER CITY*

EXPENSIVE TASTES

THOMAS PARTEY'S £45 MILLION TRANSFER FROM **ATLÉTICO MADRID** TO **ARSENAL** IN 2020 MADE HIM THE MOST EXPENSIVE GHANAIAN PLAYER OF ALL TIME. FROM WHICH CLUBS WERE THE FOLLOWING SIGNED?

1 **NICOLAS PÉPÉ** -- £72,000,000 IN 2019

2 **PIERRE-EMERICK AUBAMEYANG** -- £56,000,000 IN 2018

3 **BEN WHITE** -- £50,000,000 IN 2021

4 **ALEXANDRE LACAZETTE** -- £46,500,000 IN 2017

5 **MESUT ÖZIL** -- £42,500,000 IN 2013

6 **GRANIT XHAKA** -- £38,000,000 IN 2019

7 **SHKODRAN MUSTAFI** -- £35,000,000 IN 2016

8 **MARTIN ØDEGAARD** -- £34,000,000 IN 2021

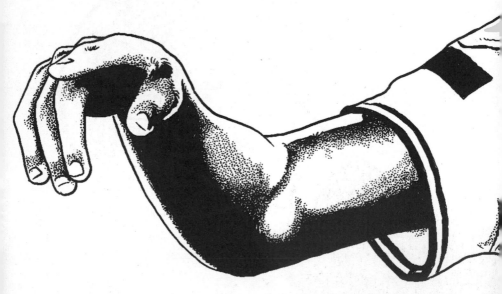

9   *ALEXIS SÁNCHEZ* --
£31,700,000 IN 2014

10   *WILLIAM SALIBA* --
£27,000,000 IN 2018

CATALAN CONNECTIONS

A PRODUCT OF **LA MASIA, BARCELONA'S** CELEBRATED YOUTH ACADEMY, **CESC FÀBREGAS** SPENT EIGHT SEASONS WITH **THE GUNNERS** DURING WHICH HE ESTABLISHED HIMSELF AS ONE OF THE BEST MIDFIELDERS IN THE WORLD. AFTER A PROTRACTED TRANSFER SAGA, HE REJOINED **BARCELONA** IN 2011, FOR AN INITIAL FEE OF €29 MILLION WITH A FURTHER €5 MILLION IN ADD-ONS, PLUS HE WOULD PAY **ARSENAL** €1 MILLION A YEAR FROM HIS WAGES FOR FIVE YEARS.

IDENTIFY THESE OTHERS WITH **ARSENAL** AND **BARCELONA** LINKS:

1 **CAMEROON** INTERNATIONAL MIDFIELDER WHO LEFT **ARSENAL** FOR **BARCELONA** IN 2012 IN A £15 MILLION TRANSFER, HE WON LA LIGA IN HIS DEBUT SEASON AND LATER PLAYED FOR **WEST HAM UNITED** ON LOAN.

2 AFTER SIGNING HIM AS A TEEN FROM **MANCHESTER CITY** IN 2013, **BARCELONA** LOANED HIM OUT TO **SEVILLA**, SOLD HIM TO **VILLARREAL** THEN BOUGHT HIM BACK AND LOANED HIM TO **ARSENAL**, BEFORE SELLING HIM TO **CELTA VIGO** IN 2019.

3 CHILEAN WHO WON LA LIGA AND NUMEROUS HONOURS WITH **BARCELONA**, TWO FA CUPS WITH **ARSENAL**, FLOPPED AT **MANCHESTER UNITED** AND THEN WON SERIE A WITH **INTERNAZIONALE**.

4 **BELGIUM** CENTRAL DEFENDER WHO SPENT FIVE SEASONS WITH **ARSENAL** BEFORE JOINING **BARCELONA** IN 2014, LATER PLAYING FOR **ROMA** AND **VISSEL KOBE**.

5 BRAZILIAN FULL BACK WHO HAD TWO SEASONS WITH **ARSENAL**, WON THREE LEAGUE TITLES AND TWO CHAMPIONS LEAGUES WITH **BARCELONA**, THEN HAD A SEASON WITH **MANCHESTER CITY**.

6 SIX-TIME BELARUSSIAN FOOTBALLER OF THE YEAR, HE JOINED **BARCELONA** FROM **ARSENAL** IN 2008 AND WON A LEAGUE, CUP AND CHAMPIONS LEAGUE TREBLE IN HIS DEBUT SEASON, WON A LEAGUE CUP ON LOAN TO **BIRMINGHAM CITY** IN 2010 AND LATER PLAYED IN GERMANY, RUSSIA, BELARUS AND TURKEY.

7 **NETHERLANDS** INTERNATIONAL WINGER WHO WON MULTIPLE HONOURS WITH **AJAX**, INCLUDING THREE LEAGUE TITLES AND THE CHAMPIONS LEAGUE, THEN WON THE DOUBLE WITH **ARSENAL** IN 1998, BEFORE SPENDING FOUR SEASONS WITH **BARCELONA**.

8 WORLD CUP AND EUROS WINNER WHO WON LEAGUE AND CUP HONOURS WITH BOTH **MONACO** AND **ARSENAL**, THEN SPENT A SEASON AT **BARCELONA** BEFORE JOINING **CHELSEA**.

9 HE WON HONOURS WITH **FRANCE**, **MONACO**, **ARSENAL**, **BARCELONA** AND **NEW YORK RED BULLS**.

10 CAPPED 106 TIMES BY THE **NETHERLANDS**, HE WON HONOURS WITH **FEYENOORD**, **RANGERS**, **ARSENAL** AND **BARCELONA**.

BIG BOSS BERTIE!

BERTIE MEE'S PLAYING CAREER WAS LIMITED, BY INJURY AND THE SECOND WORLD WAR, TO A HANDFUL OF APPEARANCES FOR **DERBY COUNTY** AND **MANSFIELD TOWN**. AFTER SERVING WITH THE ROYAL ARMY MEDICAL CORPS HE TRAINED AS A PHYSIOTHERAPIST, AND IT WAS IN THAT CAPACITY THAT HE JOINED **ARSENAL** IN 1960. WHEN **BILLY WRIGHT** WAS SACKED IN 1966, **MEE** WAS THE SURPRISING CHOICE TO REPLACE HIM. TO COMPENSATE FOR HIS LACK OF TACTICAL KNOWLEDGE, **MEE** RECRUITED COACHES **DAVE SEXTON** AND **DON HOWE** ... AND STEERED **ARSENAL** TO THEIR FIRST TROPHIES SINCE THE EARLY 1950S!

IDENTIFY THE **ARSENAL** MANAGERS BY THE CLUBS THEY PLAYED FOR:

1 CHELSEA, BRENTFORD, MANCHESTER UNITED, SHEFFIELD UNITED, COLCHESTER UNITED

2 KIVETON PARK, ASHTON NORTH END, STALYBRIDGE ROVERS, ROCHDALE, GRIMSBY TOWN, SWINDON TOWN, SHEPPEY UNITED, WORKSOP TOWN, NORTHAMPTON TOWN, SHEFFIELD UNITED, NOTTS COUNTY, TOTTENHAM HOTSPUR

3 HALMSTAD, ARSENAL, WEST HAM UNITED, SEATTLE SOUNDERS, CHICAGO FIRE, CELTIC, SHIMIZU S-PULSE, MUMBAI CITY

4 WOLVERHAMPTON WANDERERS

5 ROTHERHAM UNITED, BRADFORD CITY, ARSENAL, PETERBOROUGH UNITED

6 MUTZIG, MULHOUSE, ASPV STRASBOURG, RC STRASBOURG

7 LUTON TOWN, ASTON VILLA, DERBY COUNTY, EVERTON, BIRMINGHAM CITY, SHEFFIELD UNITED, SEATTLE SOUNDERS, TORQUAY UNITED

8 ASTON VILLA, CHELSEA, ARSENAL, MANCHESTER UNITED, PORTSMOUTH, CRYSTAL PALACE, CALIFORNIA SURF

9 REAL SOCIEDAD, TOLEDO, RACING FERROL, LEGANÉS, LORCA DEPORTIVA

10 WEST BROMWICH ALBION, ARSENAL

11 BARCELONA, PARIS SAINT-GERMAIN, RANGERS, REAL SOCIEDAD, EVERTON, ARSENAL

12 BRIGHTON & HOVE ALBION

13 ARSENAL, HULL CITY

DAD AND LAD

HAVING LAUNCHED HIS CAREER AT *STOCKPORT COUNTY* -- WHERE HE ACTUALLY PLAYED IN THE SAME TEAM AS HIS DAD -- *DAVID HERD* MADE HIS NAME AT *ARSENAL*, FINISHING AS THE CLUB'S TOP SCORER FOUR SEASONS IN A ROW. HE JOINED *MANCHESTER UNITED* IN A £35,000 DEAL IN 1961, GOING ON TO WIN TWO LEAGUE TITLES AND THE FA CUP. HE WAS A SQUAD MEMBER WHEN *UNITED* WON THE EUROPEAN CUP IN 1968. CAPPED FIVE TIMES BY *SCOTLAND*, HE LATER PLAYED FOR *STOKE CITY* AND *WATERFORD* AND MANAGED *LINCOLN CITY*.

IDENTIFY THESE OTHER DADS AND LADS WITH *ARSENAL* LINKS:

1 SON OF *JOE*, AN *ENGLAND* DEFENDER WHO SPENT 19 YEARS AT *FULHAM*, A RIGHT-BACK WHO WAS WITH *ARSENAL* FOR SIX YEARS BEFORE JOINING *MANCHESTER CITY* IN 1964. AFTER HELPING THE CLUB SECURE PROMOTION TO THE TOP FLIGHT, HE PLAYED FOR *READING* BEFORE HIS CAREER TOOK HIM TO IRELAND.

2 SON OF *ENGLAND* WINGER *MARK*, WHOSE CLUBS INCLUDED *PORT VALE*, *STOKE CITY*, *SHEFFIELD WEDNESDAY* AND *PORTSMOUTH*, AN *ENGLAND* INTERNATIONAL WHO JOINED *ARSENAL* FROM *SOUTHAMPTON*, AND WON THREE FA CUPS BEFORE SIGNING FOR *LIVERPOOL* IN 2017.

3 MIDFIELDER WHOSE CLUBS INCLUDE *ARSENAL*, *WEST BROMWICH ALBION*, *SWANSEA CITY* AND *EXETER CITY*, HIS SON *ETHAN* IS A *WALES* INTERNATIONAL WHO WAS *EXETER'S* YOUNGEST-EVER PLAYER BEFORE JOINING *CHELSEA* IN 2017.

4 SIGNED FROM *BORUSSIA DORTMUND* IN 2018, HE IS APPROACHING THE TALLY OF 80 *GABON* CAPS THAT HIS FATHER, *PIERRE-FRANÇOIS*, WON IN THE 1980S AND '90S.

5 SON OF A FORMER *SOUTHPORT* PLAYER WHO MANAGED *HALIFAX TOWN*, *PRESTON NORTH END* AND A NUMBER OF SWEDISH CLUBS BEFORE BEING KILLED IN A CAR CRASH IN CYPRUS IN 1982.

6 HIS SON, *DEVANTE*, HAS PLAYED FOR *MANCHESTER CITY*, *BRADFORD CITY*, *MOTHERWELL*, *BARNSLEY* AND MORE.

7 ENGLAND DEFENDER WHOSE SON, *NIALL*, LAUNCHED HIS CAREER AT *READING*, PLAYED FOR PARTICK THISTLE AND WON TWO *REPUBLIC OF IRELAND U21* CAPS IN 2016.

8 TWO OF HIS SONS ENJOYED GREAT PROFESSIONAL CAREERS, BOTH STARTING OUT AT *MANCHESTER CITY* AND BOTH LATER PLAYING FOR *NEW YORK RED BULLS*.

9 THREE-TIMES CZECH FOOTBALLER OF THE YEAR WHO FOLLOWED IN THE FOOTSTEPS OF HIS FATHER, *JIŘÍ*, BY PLAYING FOR *SPARTA PRAGUE*.

10 *ARSENAL* WINGER WHO LATER CHAIRED THE *PFA* BEFORE BECOMING A *MANCHESTER CITY* EXECUTIVE. HIS SON, *JAMES*, PLAYED FOR *GATESHEAD*, *ST. MIRREN* AND MORE.

LEADERS OF MEN

HAVING CAPTAINED *THE GUNNERS* ON HIS 20TH BIRTHDAY DURING AN END-OF-SEASON TOUR IN 1962, *TERRY NEILL* WAS APPOINTED TO THE ROLE PERMANENTLY -- AND AT 20 YEARS AND 102 DAYS, REMAINS THE YOUNGEST CAPTAIN IN *ARSENAL* HISTORY.

HOW MANY OF *NEILL'S* SUCCESSORS AS CAPTAIN CAN YOU NAME?

1 1963-66: HAD GONE ON STRIKE TO JOIN *ARSENAL* AND SUED *NEWCASTLE UNITED* FOR RESTRAINT OF TRADE.

2 1966-67: *ENGLAND* FULL-BACK WHO WENT ON TO MANAGE *ARSENAL* IN THE 1980S.

3 1967-73: LED *ARSENAL* TO THE 1971 DOUBLE, THE SAME YEAR HE WAS VOTED FWA PLAYER OF THE YEAR AND MADE AN MBE.

4 1973-74: SIGNED FROM *HUDDERSFIELD TOWN*, *ENGLAND* FULL-BACK WHO BECAME A SUCCESSFUL U.S. PROPERTY DEVELOPER.

5 1975-76: SCOTTISH MIDFIELDER WHO WENT ON TO PLAY FOR *QUEENS PARK RANGERS*, *LEICESTER CITY*, *NOTTS COUNTY*, *BOURNEMOUTH*, *KETTERING TOWN* AND *TORQUAY UNITED*.

6 1975-77: WORLD CUP-WINNING MIDFIELDER.

7 1976-80: WENT ON TO MANAGE *ARSENAL* FOR 2 WEEKS, 3 DAYS.

8 1980-83: HOLDS *ARSENAL'S* ALL-TIME APPEARANCE RECORD.

9 1983-86: SUBSEQUENTLY DISGRACED *ENGLAND* MIDFIELDER.

10 1986-88: *ENGLAND'S* SECOND MOST CAPPED FULL-BACK.

11 1987-2002: CAPTAINED TITLE-WINNERS IN THREE DIFFERENT DECADES.

12 2002-05: 1998 WORLD CUP AND EURO 2000 WINNER.

13 2005-07: *ARSENAL'S* ALL-TIME LEADING GOALSCORER.

14 2007-08: FRENCH CENTRAL DEFENDER STRIPPED OF THE CAPTAINCY AFTER PUBLICLY CRITICISING TEAMMATES.

15 2008-11: SPANIARD WHOSE CAPTAINCY ENDED WHEN HE SIGNED FOR **BARCELONA**.

16 2011-12: HIS CAPTAINCY ENDED WHEN HE JOINED **MANCHESTER UNITED**.

17 2012-14: BELGIAN WHOSE CAPTAINCY ENDED WHEN HE SIGNED FOR **BARCELONA**.

18 2014-16: SPANIARD WHO MADE SIX LEAGUE STARTS IN HIS FIRST YEAR AS CAPTAIN AND THEN NONE AT ALL IN HIS SECOND.

19 2016-18: GERMAN WHO MADE TWO APPEARANCES IN HIS FIRST SEASON AS CAPTAIN AND 12 IN HIS SECOND.

20 2018-19: FRENCHMAN WHO WENT ON STRIKE AT THE END OF HIS FIRST SEASON AS CAPTAIN TO FORCE A MOVE TO **BORDEAUX**.

21 2019-20: HIS TENURE ENDED AFTER HE REACTED ANGRILY TO BEING BOOED AND JEERED BY **ARSENAL** FANS AS HE LEFT THE PITCH.

22 2019: FRANCE-BORN **GABON** STRIKER.

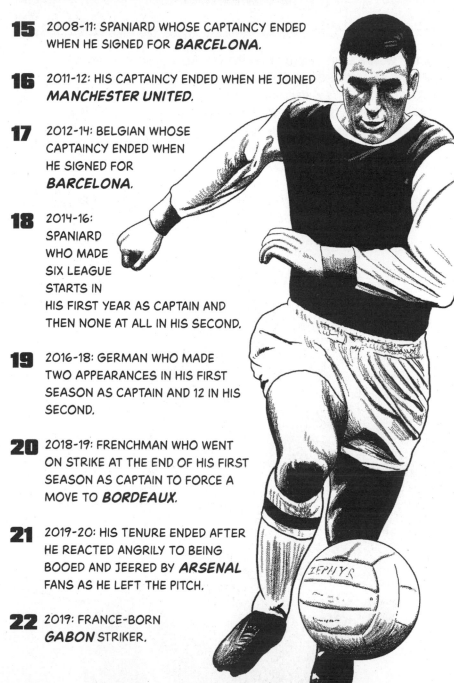

BOUND FOR FOREIGN CLIMES

HAVING WON A LEAGUE CUP WITH *ARSENAL* IN 1987, *REPUBLIC OF IRELAND* STRIKER *NIALL QUINN* SPENT SEVEN SEASONS WITH *MANCHESTER CITY*, BEFORE JOINING *SUNDERLAND*, WHERE HIS STRIKING PARTNERSHIP WITH *KEVIN PHILLIPS* WAS ONE OF THE MOST PROLIFIC THE PREMIER LEAGUE HAS SEEN. *QUINN* HAD A BRIEF SPELL PLAYING IN THAILAND WITH BANGKOK SIDE *BEC TERO SASANA* BEFORE HANGING UP HIS PLAYING BOOTS.

IDENTIFY THE COUNTRY IN WHICH THE FOLLOWING *GUNNERS* EITHER PLAYED FOR OR COACHED THE LISTED TEAM:

1 *LEN JULIANS -- GOR MAHIA* (1983-87, 1991)

2 *FRANCIS JEFFERS -- FLORIANA* (2012)

3 *PAUL DAVIS -- STABÆK* (1995)

4 *CHARLIE GEORGE -- BULOVA* (1981-82)

5 *TONY ADAMS -- GABALA* (2010-11)

6 *JAY BOTHROYD -- MUANGTHONG UNITED* (2014)

7 *ALAN BALL -- FLOREAT ATHENA* (1982)

8 *PAUL MARINER -- NAXXAR LIONS* (1990-91)

9 *GUS CAESAR -- SING TAO* (1997-99)

10 *CHRISTOPHER WREH -- PERSEMAN MANOKWARI* (2007-2010)

11 *ROBERT PIRES -- FC GOA* (2014-15)

12 *ANDREY ARSHAVIN -- KAIRAT* (2016-18)

LILYWHITE GUNNERS

CONTROVERSIAL **TOGO** STRIKER **EMMANUEL ADEBAYOR'S** CAREER PATH TOOK HIM FROM **MONACO** TO **ARSENAL**, **MANCHESTER CITY**, **REAL MADRID**, **TOTTENAM HOTSPUR**, **CRYSTAL PALACE** AND CLUBS IN TURKEY AND PARAGUAY.

IDENTIFY THESE OTHERS WHO HAVE PLAYED FOR **ARSENAL** AND **SPURS**:

1 HAVING CAPTAINED *GREAT BRITAIN* AT THE 1960 OLYMPICS, HE JOINED *ARSENAL* FROM *NORTHAMPTON TOWN* IN 1961, BEFORE MOVING ON TO ARCH-RIVALS *TOTTENHAM HOTSPUR* THREE YEARS LATER IN A £40,000 DEAL.

2 *SCOTLAND* CENTRE-HALF WHO FOLLOWED MANAGER *TERRY NEILL* FROM *TOTTENHAM* TO *ARSENAL* IN 1977.

3 FORMER *TOTTENHAM, LEYTON ORIENT* AND *ARSENAL* INSIDE-FORWARD WHOSE NEPHEW, *PERRY*, ALSO PLAYED FOR *ARSENAL*.

4 FRENCH CENTRE-BACK WHO PLAYED FOR *CHELSEA, ARSENAL* AND *SPURS* BETWEEN 2001 AND 2013.

5 *ENGLAND* CENTRAL DEFENDER WHO, HAVING WON THE LEAGUE CUP WITH *SPURS* IN 1999, WON TWO LEAGUE TITLES AND THREE FA CUPS WITH *ARSENAL* -- INCLUDING THE DOUBLE IN 2002 -- BEFORE JOINING *PORTSMOUTH*, WITH WHOM HE WON THE FA CUP IN 2008. HE ENJOYED A LAST HURRAH AT *ARSENAL* IN 2010, AFTER WHICH HE ENDED HIS PLAYING CAREER AT *NEWCASTLE UNITED*.

6 *ARSENAL* YOUNGSTER WHOSE NOMADIC CAREER TOOK HIM TO *NORWICH CITY, BLACKBURN ROVERS, SPURS, BIRMINGHAM CITY, WEST HAM UNITED* AND *FC ROSTOV*, BEFORE HE PACKED IN THE GAME AT THE AGE OF 29.

7 SCOTTISH WINGER WHO, HAVING WON THE FA CUP WITH *SPURS* IN 1967, JOINED *ARSENAL* THE NEXT YEAR IN A STRAIGHT SWAP FOR *DAVID JENKINS*. HE WENT ON TO PLAY FOR *BOBBY ROBSON'S IPSWICH TOWN* AND *TONY WADDINGTON'S STOKE CITY*.

8 GOALKEEPER CAPPED 119 TIMES BY *NORTHERN IRELAND*.

TURKISH DELIGHTS

HAVING WON HONOURS WITH **FEYENOORD, ARSENAL** AND **MANCHESTER UNITED, ROBIN VAN PERSIE** JOINED **FENERBAHÇE** THREE WEEKS BEFORE HIS 32ND BIRTHDAY IN 2015. THE INJURY WOES THAT HAD PLAGUED HIM AT **OLD TRAFFORD** CONTINUED THROUGHOUT HIS TIME IN TURKEY AND HE REJOINED **FEYENOORD** IN EARLY 2018 FOR AN 18-MONTH SWANSONG THAT EARNED HIM KNVB CUP AND JOHAN CRUYFF SHIELD MEDALS.

WHICH TURKISH CLUBS DID THE FOLLOWING **GUNNERS** SIGN FOR?

1   **MESUT ÖZIL** -- 2021

2   **JUNICHI INAMOTO** -- 2008

3   **EMMANUEL ADEBAYOR** -- A) 2017   B) 2019

4   **NICOLAS ANELKA** -- 2005

5   **GAËL CLICHY** -- 2017

6   **ARMAND TRAORÉ** -- 2018

7   **SAMIR NASRI** -- 2017

8   **KEVIN CAMPBELL** -- 1998

9   **LUKAS PODOLSKI** -- A) 2015   B) 2020

10   **OĞUZHAN ÖZYAKUP** -- 2015

11   **ANDRÉ SANTOS** -- A) 2009   B) 2016

WELL I NEVER ...

DENNIS BERGKAMP'S NICKNAME AT *ARSENAL* WAS THE *"NON-FLYING DUTCHMAN"* BECAUSE OF A PHOBIA THAT PREVENTED HIM TRAVELLING BY AIR. SPEAKING OF ODDBALL FACTS:

1 WHICH LONDONER, ON MAKING HIS DEBUT FOR THE *REPUBLIC OF IRELAND* IN 1973, COMPLAINED TO A TEAMMATE ABOUT THE LENGTH OF THE OPPOSITION'S NATIONAL ANTHEM ... ONLY TO BE INFORMED THAT IT WAS ACTUALLY THE IRISH ANTHEM?

2 WHICH FORMER *ARSENAL* STAR IS SAID TO BE WORTH AS MUCH AS £20 BILLION AFTER FOUNDING A BIOCHEMICALS COMPANY?

3 IN 2021, WHICH FORMER *ARSENAL* PLAYER OPENED A RESTAURANT IN PARIS CALLED *AMERICAN TASTY BURGER?*

4 WHEN HE TOOK THE FIELD TO MAKE HIS *GUNNERS* DEBUT, AWAY TO *LEEDS UNITED* IN 1992, WHO BECAME THE FIRST-EVER *ARSENAL* GOALKEEPER TO COME ON AS A SUBSTITUTE?

5 IN 2001, WHILE ON THE BOOKS AT *WATFORD*, WHICH FORMER *ARSENAL* MIDFIELDER WAS STABBED BY AN INTRUDER AT HIS ISLINGTON HOME, IN AN INCIDENT THAT SAW FELLOW *ARSENAL* TRAINEE *ANDREW DOUGLAS* CRITICALLY INJURED?

6 WHICH *ARSENAL* GREAT ACCEPTED A SMUGGLED CORN ON THE COB FROM FELLOW CONTESTANT *CAITLYN JENNER* ON SEASON 19 OF TV'S *"I'M A CELEBRITY...GET ME OUT OF HERE!"?*

7 WHICH MIDFIELDER, WHO WON A LEAGUE TITLE WITH *THE GUNNERS* IN 1991 AND LATER PLAYED FOR *PORTSMOUTH* AND *BRISTOL ROVERS*, BECAME A BRISTOL FIREMAN AFTER HIS PLAYING DAYS WERE OVER?

8 WHICH *ARSENAL* PLAYER AUTHORED A SERIES OF CHILDREN'S BOOKS FEATURING HERO *T.J.* AND HIS SCHOOL FOOTBALL TEAM?

9 WHICH ERSTWHILE *ARSENAL* GOALKEEPER ONCE INJURED HIMSELF PUTTING HIS SUITCASES AWAY IN THE LOFT?

10 WHICH FORMER **ARSENAL** STAR, WHILE
PLAYING FOR **SOUTHAMPTON**, MANAGED
TO AMPUTATE HIS INDEX FINGER AND LOP OFF
THE TIP OF ANOTHER WHEN HE TANGLED
WITH HIS LAWNMOWER?

THE VIP SECTION

ARSENAL FAN **IDRIS ELBA** ONCE SAID ON BBC FOOTBALL FOCUS THAT IF **SPURS** WON THE LEAGUE HE'D BE **"PHYSICALLY ILL, LITERALLY THROWING UP"**. IDENTIFY THESE OTHER CELEBRITY GOONERS:

1   ACTOR WHO PLAYED **JONATHAN CREEK** ON TV.

2   REAL NAME **FLORIAN CLOUD DE BOUNEVIALLE O'MALLEY ARMSTRONG**, SHE HIT THE POP CHARTS WITH HITS INCLUDING **"HERE WITH ME"**, **"THANK YOU"** AND **"WHITE FLAG"**.

3   LEAD SINGER WITH **THE SEX PISTOLS** AND **PUBLIC IMAGE LTD**.

4   ONE HALF OF **THE PET SHOP BOYS** WITH **NEIL TENNANT**.

5   ACTOR WHO PLAYS **TED HASTINGS** ON TV'S **"LINE OF DUTY"**.

6   **SPANDAU BALLET** BASSIST WHO PLAYED **STEVE OWEN** ON THE BBC TV SOAP OPERA **"EASTENDERS"**.

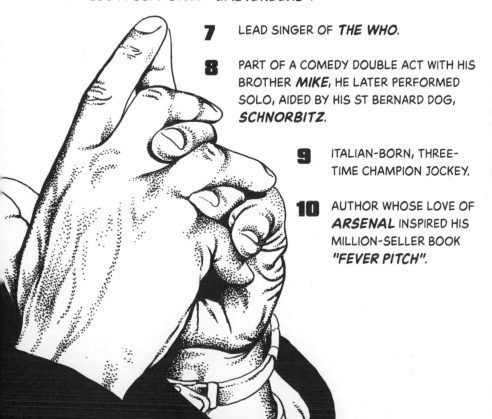

7   LEAD SINGER OF **THE WHO**.

8   PART OF A COMEDY DOUBLE ACT WITH HIS BROTHER **MIKE**, HE LATER PERFORMED SOLO, AIDED BY HIS ST BERNARD DOG, **SCHNORBITZ**.

9   ITALIAN-BORN, THREE-TIME CHAMPION JOCKEY.

10   AUTHOR WHOSE LOVE OF **ARSENAL** INSPIRED HIS MILLION-SELLER BOOK **"FEVER PITCH"**.

1001 ANSWERS

The French Connection (pg 02)

1. Bacary Sagna   2. Laurent Koscielny   3. Mathieu Flamini
4. Mikaël Silvestre   5. William Gallas   6. Sébastien Squillaci
7. Francis Coquelin   8. Gilles Grimandi   9. Robert Pirès
10. Sylvain Wiltord

Euro Hero (pg 04)

1. Everton   2. Crystal Palace
3. FC Köln   4. Nottingham Forest
5. Liverpool   6. Manchester United   7. Everton   8. Bari
9. Tottenham Hotspur
10. Ipswich Town   11. Chelsea
12. Manchester United

The Blues Brothers (pg 06)

1. Matthew Upson   2. David Seaman   3. Nicklas Bendtner
4. Krystian Bielik   5. Carl Jenkinson   6. Christopher Wreh
7. Sebastian Larsson   8. David Bentley   9. Johan Djourou
10. Jermaine Pennant

Eagles Have Landed (pg 08)

1. Clive Allen   2. Ian Wright
3. Paul Dickov   4. Ashley Cole
5. Eddie McGoldrick
6. Kenny Sansom

Red & White Dragons (pg 10)

1. Mike Smith, Mike England, David Williams, Terry Yorath
2. Mel Charles   3. Aaron Ramsey
4. Walley Barnes   5. John Hartson   6. Dave Bowen
7. Bobby Gould   8. Jack Kelsey

Biting the Hand That Fed Them (pg 12)

1. Emmanuel Adebayor
2. Giovanni van Bronckhorst
3. Andy Cole   4. Robin van Persie
5. Cesc Fàbregas   6. Unai Emery
7. George Graham
8. Nicolas Anelka

"Mr. Arsenal" (pg 14)

1. Terry Neill, Don Howe, Steve Burtenshaw, George Graham, Stewart Houston, Bruce Rioch, Pat Rice, Arsène Wenger
2. Bobby Robson   3. Glenn Hoddle   4. Kevin Keegan
5. David Platt   6. Wycombe Wanderers   7. Portsmouth
8. Azerbaijan   9. Granada   10. 6

The Boys of 1994 (pg 16)

1. Manchester City   2. Retired
3. West Ham United   4. Stabæk
5. Sunderland   6. Retired
7. Nottingham Forest
8. Queens Park Rangers
9. Retired   10. Middlesbrough
11. Fulham   12. Crystal Palace
13. Middlesbrough 14. Manchester City   15. Middlesbrough
16. Manchester City

The Russians are Coming! (pg 18)

1. Alexander Hleb   2. Emmanuel Frimpong   3. David Bentley
4. Kim Källström   5. Unai Emery
6. Quincy Owusu-Abeyie
7. Alex Song

Gunners and Hammers (pg 20)

1. Manuel Almunia 2. Kaba Diawara 3. Luís Boa Morte 4. Jérémie Aliadière 5. John Radford 6. Davor Šuker 7. Yossi Benayoun

The Young Ones (pg 22)

1. Jack Wilshere 2. Jermaine Pennant 3. Paul Vaessen 4. Gerry Ward 5. Bukayo Saka 6. Nicklas Bendtner 7. Aaron Ramsey 8. John Radford

Pokal Power! (pg 24)

1. Bayern Munich 2. Werder Bremen 3. Wolfsburg 4. Borussia Dortmund 5. Borussia Dortmund 6. Bayern Munich

Going Dutch (pg 26)

1. Dennis Bergkamp 2. Giovanni van Bronckhorst 3. Glenn Helder 4. Gerrit Keizer 5. Thomas Vermaelen 6. Ryo Miyaichi 7. Yaya Sanogo 8. Marc Overmars

Saintly Boys (pg 28)

1. Alan Ball 2. Alex Oxlade-Chamberlain 3. Charlie George 4. Steve Williams 5. Calum Chambers 6. Walley Barnes 7. Perry Groves 8. Ted Drake 9. Cédric Soares 10. Luís Boa Morte

Pépé La Whoo!!! (pg 30)

1. Lille 2. Cameroon 3. a) Marouane Chamakh b) Gervinho c) Pierre-Emerick Aubameyang 4. Pierre-Emerick Aubameyang 5. Unai Emery 6. 19 7. Aston Villa 8. Ezgjan Alioski

Working for the Man! (pg 32)

1. Real Madrid 2. Manchester City 3. Bolton Wanderers 4. Real Madrid 5. Chelsea 6. Bolton Wanderers 7. Shanghai Shenhua 8. Liverpool 9. Chelsea 10. Mumbai City FC 11. West Bromwich Albion 12. Paris Saint-Germain 13. Fenerbahçe 14. Chelsea

The Hornets' Nest (pg 34)

1. Mart Poom 2. Héctor Bellerín 3. Pat Jennings 4. Brian Talbot 5. Pat Rice 6. Kevin Richardson 7. Danny Welbeck

"Kenny White Shorts" (pg 36)

1. Crystal Palace 2. Terry Neill 3. Clive Allen 4. Liverpool 5. Newcastle United 6. Queens Park Rangers 7. Terry Butcher, Don Howe, Bobby Gould 8. Everton 9. Watford 10. Ron Greenwood, Bobby Robson

Kings of Europe! (pg 38)
1. Barcelona   2. Liverpool
3. Chelsea   4. Ajax   5. Real
Madrid   6. Bayern Munich
7. Barcelona
8. Manchester United
9. Barcelona   10. Real Madrid
11. Chelsea   12. Manchester United
and Aston Villa   13. Barcelona
14. Barcelona   15. Nottingham
Forest   16. Liverpool
17. Manchester United   18. Ajax

Legendary Lawton (pg 40)
1. Sheffield Wednesday
2. West Bromwich Albion
3. Everton   4. Manchester City
5. Preston North End
6. Manchester United
7. Manchester United
8. Manchester United
9. Liverpool   10. Manchester
United   11. Manchester City
12. Chelsea   13. Chelsea
14. Liverpool

Captains Fantastic (pg 42)
1. Alex James   2. Joe Mercer
3. Frank McLintock   4. Pat Rice
5. Tony Adams   6. Tony Adams
7. Tony Adams   8. David Seaman
9. Patrick Vieira   10. Mikel Arteta
11. Per Mertesacker
12. Per Mertesacker
13. Pierre-Emerick Aubameyang

City Slickers (pg 44)
1. Sylvinho   2. Paul Dickov
3. David Seaman   4. Dave
Bacuzzi   5. Emmanuel Adebayor
6. Bacary Sagna   7. Kolo Touré
8. David Rocastle   9. Niall Quinn
10. Patrick Vieira

Young Guns Gunners! (pg 46)
1. Tony Woodcock   2. Tony
Adams   3. Paul Merson
4. Cesc Fàbregas
5. Jack Wilshere

An All-Time High! (pg 48)
1. Thierry Henry   2. Robin van
Persie   3. Alexis Sánchez
4. Davor Šuker   5. Emmanuel
Adebayor   6. Henrikh Mkhitaryan
7. Pierre-Emerick Aubameyang
8. Niall Quinn   9. Frank Stapleton

Old Boys and "The Old Lady" (pg 50)
1. Thierry Henry   2. Patrick Vieira
3. Armand Traoré   4. Nicklas
Bendtner   5. Aaron Ramsey
6. Stephan Lichtsteiner
7. Wojciech Szczęsny
8. Liam Brady

The Centurions (pg 52)
1. Barcelona   2. West Ham United
3. Retired   4. West Ham United
5. Tottenham Hotspur   6. Retired
7. Nottingham Forest
8. Manchester United   9. Retired
10. Retired   11. Retired
12. Retired   13. Fulham
14. Manchester United

15. Everton   16. Manchester United   17. Chelsea
18. Nottingham Forest

Gunners and Potters (pg 54)

1. Eddie Clamp   2. Steve Bould
3. Alan Hudson   4. George Eastham   5. Ian Allinson
6. Lee Chapman   7. David Herd
8. Matthew Upson

Ton-Up Boys (pg 56)

1. Alexis Sánchez   2. Sebastian Larsson   3. Kim Källström
4. Petr Čech   5. Thierry Henry
6. Mart Poom   7. Kolo Touré
8. Pat Jennings   9. Cesc Fàbregas   10. Olivier Giroud
11. Stephan Lichtsteiner
12. Ashley Cole   13. Patrick Vieira
14. Giovanni van Bronckhorst
15. Tomáš Rosický
16. Per Mertesacker   17. Joel Campbell   18. Robin van Persie
19. Yossi Benayoun

The Wright Stuff (pg 58)

1. Greenwich Borough   2. Mark Bright   3. Manchester United
4. Graham Taylor   5. George Graham   6. Southampton
7. Cliff Bastin   8. Harry Redknapp
9. Nottingham Forest
10. John Barnes   11. Burnley
12. Alex James

German Imports (pg 60)

1. Bayer Leverkusen
2. Werder Bremen   3. Borussia Mönchengladbach   4. Borussia Dortmund   5. Borussia Dortmund
6. 1. SC Feucht

Czech Marks (pg 62)

1. Petr Čech   2. Sparta Prague
3. Michal Papadopulos   4. John Dick   5. Slavia Prague   6. 2005
7. Glen Kamara

The Gunners and The Tricky Trees (pg 64)

1. John Barnwell   2. Kevin Campbell   3. Joe Baker   4. Aaron Ramsey   5. Willie Young   6. Colin Addison   7. Carl Jenkinson
8. Len Julians   9. Henri Lansbury

The Boys From Brazil (pg 66)

1. Gabriel   2. Denílson   3. Gabriel Paulista   4. Edu   5. Júlio Baptista
6. Gilberto Silva   7. Gabriel Martinelli   8. Willian

The Boys of 2005 (pg 68)

1. VfB Stuttgart   2. Portsmouth
3. Manchester City   4. Fulham
5. Chelsea   6. Barcelona
7. Juventus   8. Panathinaikos
9. Villarreal   10. Watford
11. Portsmouth   12. West Ham United   13. Valencia

Between the Sticks (pg 70)

1. Jim Furnell   2. Vito Mannone
3. Jimmy Rimmer   4. Bob Wilson
5. Jack Kelsey   6. David Ospina
7. Alex Manninger   8. Richard
Wright   9. Wojciech Szczęsny

Going Full Throstle! (pg 72)

1. Kieran Gibbs   2. Ainsley
Maitland-Niles   3. Don Howe
4. Serge Gnabry   5. Junichi
Inamoto   6. Alan Miller
7. Chris Whyte   8. Brian Talbot
9. Nwankwo Kanu

Making Plans For Nigel (pg 74)

1. Birmingham City, Oxford United
2. Dave Bassett   3. George
Graham   4. Bobby Robson,
Graham Taylor   5. Wimbledon
6. Dennis Irwin   7. West Ham
United   8. Blackburn Rovers

Sin Binned! (pg 76)

1. Ian Ure   2. Patrick Vieira
3. Kolo Touré   4. Lauren and
Martin Keown   5. Sol Campbell
6. Granit Xhaka   7. Alan Ball

Them's the Breaks! (pg 78)

1. Santi Cazorla   2. Abou Diaby
3. Rami Shabaan   4. Bacary
Sagna   5. Steve Morrow
6. Cesc Fàbregas   7. Jack
Wilshere   8. Aaron Ramsey

Eat Our Dust! (pg 80)

1. Aston Villa   2. Aston Villa
3. Huddersfield Town
4. Sunderland   5. Wolverhampton
Wanderers   6. Manchester United
7. Preston North End
8. Leeds United   9. Liverpool
10. Liverpool   11. Manchester
United   12. Liverpool

"Who is Messi? Who is Neymar?" (pg 82)

1. Paul Mariner   2. Niall Quinn
3. David Platt   4. Dennis
Bergkamp   5. Emmanuel Petit
6. Davor Šuker   7. Sol Campbell
8. Thierry Henry   9. Philippe
Senderos   10. Matthew Upson
11. Nicklas Bendtner
12. Giovanni van Bronckhorst
13. Mesut Özil   14. Olivier Giroud
15. Gervinho   16. Granit Xhaka

Gunners Gone Guvnors (pg 84)

1. Giovanni van Bronckhorst
2. Rémi Garde   3. Frank
McLintock   4. Bobby Gould
5. Patrick Vieira   6. Alan Ball
7. Thierry Henry   8. Dave Bowen
9. Bryan Talbot   10. Tony Adams

"Safe Hands" Seaman (pg 86)

1. Leeds United   2. Peterborough
United   3. Birmingham City
4. Jim Smith, Trevor Francis,
Don Howe   5. Bobby Robson
6. George Graham
7. Southampton   8. Manchester
City   9. Sven-Göran Eriksson
10. "Dancing on Ice"

Norn Iron Boys (pg 88)
1. Pat Jennings 2. Eddie Magill
3. Jack McClelland 4. Pat Rice
5. Daniel Ballard 6. Sammy
Nelson 7. Steve Morrow
8. Billy McCullough

Viva España! (pg 90)
1. Santi Cazorla 2. Denis Suárez
3. Cesc Fàbregas
4. Manuel Almunia 5. Pablo Marí
6. Mikel Arteta 7. Nacho Monreal

Meet the New Boss, Same as the Old Boss (pg 92)
1. Terry Neill 2. Kenny Sansom
3. Thierry Henry 4. Willie Young
5. Steve Coppell 6. Aston Villa
7. Ipswich Town 8. Coventry City
9. Peter Reid 10. Terry Venables

He's A Keeper! (pg 94)
1. Polish 2. German 3. Welsh
4. Austrian 5. Swedish
6. Estonian

Gone Too Soon (pg 96)
1. David Rocastle 2. Alan Miller
3. Niccolò Galli 4. Joe Powell
5. Tommy Caton

Nerazzurri o Rossoneri (pg 98)
1. Lukas Podolski 2. Mathieu
Flamini 3. Patrick Vieira
4. Mikaël Silvestre 5. Alexis
Sánchez 6. Nelson Vivas
7. Pierre-Emerick Aubameyang
8. Philippe Senderos 9. Olivier
Giroud 10. Nwankwo Kanu
11. Jens Lehmann 12. Liam Brady

"Shake My Little Tushy on the Catwalk ..." (pg 100)
1. Mesut Özil 2. Pat Jennings
3. Aaron Ramsey 4. John Halls
5. Ian Wright 6. Héctor Bellerín
7. Thierry Henry 8. Lukas
Podolski 9. Bob McNab

Charlie is my Darling (pg 102)
1. Ted Drake 2. Ronnie Rooke
3. Alan Smith 4. Pierre-Emerick
Aubameyang

Up for the Cup (pg 104)
1. James, Lambert 2. Lewis (2)
3. Graham, George
4. Talbot, Stapleton, Sunderland
5. Wright Replay: Wright,
Linighan 6. Overmars, Anelka
7. Parlour, Ljungberg
8. Pires 9. Cazorla, Koscielny,
Ramsey 10. Walcott, Sánchez,
Mertesacker, Giroud 11. Sánchez,
Ramsey 12. Aubameyang (2)

Pot Collectors (pg 106)
1. Manchester United 2. Everton
3. Leeds United 4. Brighton &
Hove Albion 5. Portsmouth
6. Millwall 7. Arsenal 8. Fulham
9. Manchester United
10. Manchester United
11. Liverpool 12. Sunderland
13. Chelsea 14. Blackburn Rovers
15. Stoke City 16. Leeds United
17. Leicester City

Sukerman! (pg 108)

1. Sevilla   2. Fabio Capello
3. Jupp Heynckes   4. Juventus
5. Ronaldo   6. John Toshack
7. Galatasaray
8. Harry Redknapp

Know Howe? (pg 110)

1. Vic Buckingham   2. Billy Wright
3. Dave Sexton   4. Anderlecht
5. West Bromwich Albion
6. Leeds United   7. Galatasaray
8. Terry Neill   9. Bobby Gould
10. Queens Park Rangers
11. Terry Butcher
12. Jay Bothroyd

Madridistas (pg 112)

1. Martin Ødegaard   2. Mesut
Özil   3. Nicolas Anelka   4. Júlio
Baptista   5. Dani Ceballos
6. Davor Šuker

The Italian Jobs (pg 114)

1. Roma   2. Torino   3. Napoli
4. Benevento   5. Genoa   6. Roma
7. Cremonese   8. Perugia
9. Roma   10. Udinese
11. Frosinone   12. Roma

The Old Firm (pg 116)

1. Kieran Tierney   2. Philippe
Senderos   3. Giovanni van
Bronckhorst   4. Charlie Nicholas
5. Ian Wright   6. Kolo Touré
7. Francis Jeffers   8. Tommy
Docherty   9. Freddie Ljungberg
10. Martin Hayes

Chippy's Run (pg 118)

1. Valencia   2. Michel Platini
3. Trevor Francis   4. Karl-Heinz
Rummenigge   5. Ascoli   6. John
Lyall   7. Johnny Giles, Eoin Hand,
Jack Charlton   8. Billy McNeill
9. Brighton & Hove Albion
10. Giovanni Trapattoni

PFA POTY (pg 120)

1. Pat Jennings   2. Tony
Woodcock   3. Liam Brady
4. Clive Allen   5. Tony Adams
6. Paul Merson   7. David Platt
8. Andy Cole   9. Dennis
Bergkamp   10. Thierry Henry
11. Cesc Fàbregas   12. Jack
Wilshere   13. Robin van Persie

Portuguese Geezers (pg 122)

1. Stefan Schwarz   2. Cédric
Soares   3. Rui Fonte   4. Michael
Thomas   5. Glenn Helder
6. Luís Boa Morte

There's No Business Like Show Business (pg 124)

1. Bob McNab   2. Ashley Cole
3. Sol Campbell   4. Ian Wright
5. Martin Keown   6. "Grange Hill"
7. Tommy Lawton

Not From Round Here (pg 126)

1. Finland   2. Gabon   3. Algeria
4. Ukraine   5. Latvia   6. Montserrat
7. Belarus   8. China   9. Yugoslavia
10. South Korea   11. Uruguay
12. Guinea   13. Chile   14. Colombia
15. Senegal   16. Ghana   17. Iceland

Platt's The way To Do It (pg 128)

1. Sampdoria   2. Nottingham Forest   3. Howard Wilkinson
4. Pune City

Pensioners and Gunners (pg 130)

1. Lassana Diarra   2. John Hollins
3. Tommy Docherty   4. Ashley Cole   5. David Rocastle
6. Willian

Under Spanish Skies (pg 132)

1. Villareal   2. Atlético Madrid
3. Valencia   4. Villareal
5. Valencia   6. Valencia   7. Real Sociedad   8. Real Sociedad
9. Celta de Vigo
10. Atlético Madrid
11. Real Sociedad

Brighton Peers (pg 134)

1. Danny Welbeck   2. Frank Stapleton   3. Eddie Magill
4. Martin Keown   5. Colin Pates
6. Liam Brady   7. Paul Dickov
8. Sammy Nelson

Leading by Example (pg 136)

1. Bolton Wanderers   2. Chelsea
3. Celtic   4. Real Madrid
5. Borussia Mönchengladbach
6. Lille   7. Lyon   8. Borussia Dortmund   9. Schalke 04
10. Sampdoria

Keeping Up Appearances (pg 138)

1. Tony Adams   2. George Armstrong   3. Lee Dixon
4. Nigel Winterburn   5. David Seaman   6. Pat Rice   7. Peter Storey   8. John Radford
9. Peter Simpson   10. Bob John
11. Graham Rix   12. Ray Parlour
13. Martin Keown   14. Paul Davis
15. Eddie Hapgood   16. Paul Merson   17. Dennis Bergkamp
18. Patrick Vieira
19. Frank McLintock

"The Boys From The Mersey ..." (pg 140)

1. Alex Manninger   2. Jermaine Pennant   3. Yossi Benayoun
4. Geoff Strong   5. Kolo Touré
6. Ray Kennedy   7. Jim Furnell
8. Nicolas Anelka

"...and The Thames ..." (pg 142)

1. Switzerland   2. Peter Storey
3. Moritz Volz   4. Luís Boa Morte
5. Junichi Inamoto   6. Malcolm Macdonald   7. Andy Cole
8. Calum Chambers

"... and The Tyne" (pg 144)

1. Joe Willock   2. Sol Campbell
3. Andy Cole   4. Ray Bowden
5. Mathieu Debuchy   6. Malcolm Macdonald   7. Pat Howard
8. George Eastham   9. Alex Cropley   10. Bob Benson

The Boys of 1979 (pg 146)

1. Watford   2. Brighton & Hove Albion   3. Watford   4. Leeds United   5. Nottingham Forest   6. Juventus   7. Ipswich Town   8. Manchester United   9. Crystal Palace   10. Caen   11. Norwich City

Bad Boys! Bad Boys! (pg 148)

1. Wojciech Szczęsny   2. Willie Young   3. Paul Vaessen   4. Edu   5. Jermaine Pennant   6. Nicklas Bendtner   7. Peter Storey   8. Samir Nasri   9. Tony Adams   10. Ian Wright

Stroller's Pace (pg 150)

1. Joe Mercer   2. Tommy Docherty   3. Leicester City   4. Tommy Docherty   5. Frank O'Farrell   6. Portsmouth, Crystal Palace, California Surf   7. Millwall   8. Accepting payments from a football agent whose clients had been signed by Arsenal   9. Leeds United   10. Tottenham Hotspur

The Front Man (pg 152)

1. Tony Waiters   2. Bobby Robson   3. Don Revie   4. Arsenal   5. AZ '67   6. Don Howe   7. Alan Ball   8. Steve Nicol   9. Peter Reid   10. Toronto FC

"Celebrate Good Times ... Come On!" (pg 154)

1. Watford   2. Wolverhampton Wanderers   3. Fulham   4. Queens Park Rangers   5. New England Tea Men   6. Leicester City   7. Manchester United   8. West Ham United   9. Liverpool   10. Birmingham City   11. Leicester City

"I've Got the Music in Me!" (pg 156)

1. Alexis Sánchez   2. Ian Wright   3. Andy Cole   4. Jimmy Hill   5. "Hot Stuff"   6. Quincy Owusu-Abeyie

"Life Is So Good In America ..." (pg 158)

1. Terry Mancini   2. Bacary Sagna   3. Kieran Gibbs   4. Brian Kidd   5. Steve Morrow   6. Charlie George   7. Mikaël Silvestre   8. Ashley Cole   9. Alan Ball   10. Thierry Henry

Supermac (pg 160)

1. Bobby Robson   2. Luton Town   3. Joe Harvey   4. Cyprus   5. Terry Neill   6. Ronnie Rooke   7. Djurgården   8. Fulham   9. Huddersfield Town

Paddy Powerful! (pg 162)

1. AS Cannes   2. Marcel Desailly   3. Rémi Garde   4. Three   5. Fabio Capello   6. José Mourinho, Roberto Mancini   7. Roberto Mancini   8. Stoke City   9. New York City FC   10. Nice   11. Roy Hodgson

Lucky Number 9? (pg 164)
1. Lucas Pérez   2. Eduardo da Silva   3. Júlio Baptista
4. Francis Jeffers   5. Davor Šuker

Money Matters (pg 166)
1. Tommy Docherty
2. Mel Charles   3. George Eastham   4. Joe Baker   5. Frank McLintock   6. Bobby Gould
7. Peter Marinello   8. Alan Ball
9. Brian Talbot   10. Kenny Sansom   11. Ian Wright
12. Dennis Bergkamp
13. Thierry Henry   14. Sylvain Wiltord   15. Lucas Torreira

Land of the Rising Sun (pg 168)
1. Thomas Vermaelen   2. Ryo Miyaichi   3. Jay Bothroyd
4. Nagoya Grampus Eight
5. Takuma Asano   6. Junichi Inamoto   7. Freddie Ljungberg

Oh, Danny Boy (pg 170)
1. Tottenham Hotspur   2. Preston North End   3. Steve Bruce
4. Louis van Gaal   5. Galatasaray
6. Chelsea   7. Unai Emery   8. Javi Gracia, Quique Sánchez Flores, Hayden Mullins, Nigel Pearson, Vladimir Ivić   9. Graham Potter
10. Stuart Pearce, Fabio Capello, Roy Hodgson, Gareth Southgate

Toffee Nosed (pg 172)
1. Alex Iwobi   2. Anders Limpar
3. Joe Mercer   4. Francis Jeffers
5. Richard Wright   6. Brian Kidd

South Africa (pg 174)
1. Luís Boa Morte   2. George Eastham   3. Colin Addison
4. Terry Mancini

Goals! Goals! Goals! (pg 176)
1. Ian Wright   2. Cliff Bastin
3. John Radford   4. Jimmy Brain
5. Ted Drake   6. Doug Lishman
7. Robin van Persie   8. Joe Hulme
9. David Jack

Ball of Fire! (pg 178)
1. Blackpool   2. Harry Catterick
3. West Bromwich Albion
4. Leeds United   5. Lawrie McMenemy   6. Bristol Rovers
7. Portsmouth   8. Graham Taylor
9. Southampton
10. Manchester City

Exit The Ox! (pg 180)
1. Barcelona   2. Werder Bremen
3. Panathinaikos   4. Real Sociedad   5. Fiorentina
6. Aberdeen   7. Barcelona
8. Charlton Athletic   9. Everton
10. Hamburger SV   11. Villarreal
12. Valencia   13. Roma
14. Sheffield United

Hall of Famers (pg 182)
1. Alan Ball   2. Tommy Lawton
3. Tony Adams   4. Viv Anderson
5. Alex James   6. Ian Wright
7. Liam Brady   8. Dennis Bergkamp   9. Thierry Henry
10. Cliff Bastin   11. Frank McLintock   12. Charlie Buchan
13. Patrick Vieira

Expensive Tastes (pg 184)

1. Lille   2. Borussia Dortmund
3. Brighton & Hove Albion
4. Lyon   5. Real Madrid
6. Borussia Mönchengladbach
7. Valencia   8. Real Madrid
9. Barcelona   10. Saint-Étienne

Catalan Connections (pg 186)

1. Alex Song   2. Denis Suárez
3. Alexis Sánchez   4. Thomas
Vermaelen   5. Sylvinho
6. Alexander Hleb   7. Marc
Overmars   8. Emmanuel Petit
9. Thierry Henry
10. Giovanni van Bronckhorst

Big Boss Bertie! (pg 188)

1. Stewart Houston   2. Herbert
Chapman   3. Freddie Ljungberg
4. Billy Wright
5. George Swindin   6. Arsène
Wenger   7. Bruce Rioch
8. George Graham   9. Unai Emery
10. Don Howe   11. Mikel Arteta
12. Steve Burtenshaw
13. Terry Neill

Dad and Lad (pg 190)

1. Dave Bacuzzi   2. Alex Oxlade-
Chamberlain   3. Kwame Ampadu
4. Pierre-Emerick Aubameyang
5. Alan Ball   6. Andy Cole
7. Martin Keown   8. Ian Wright
9. Tomáš Rosický
10. Brian Marwood

Leaders of Men (pg 192)

1. George Eastham   2. Don Howe
3. Frank McLintock
4. Bob McNab   5. Eddie Kelly
6. Alan Ball   7. Pat Rice   8. David
O'Leary   9. Graham Rix
10. Kenny Sansom   11. Tony
Adams   12. Patrick Vieira
13. Thierry Henry   14. William
Gallas   15. Cesc Fàbregas
16. Robin van Persie   17. Thomas
Vermaelen   18. Mikel Arteta
19. Per Mertesacker   20. Laurent
Koscielny   21. Granit Xhaka
22. Pierre-Emerick Aubameyang

Bound for Foreign Climes (pg 194)

1. Kenya   2. Malta   3. Norway
4. Hong Kong   5. Azerbaijan
6. Thailand   7. Australia   8. Malta
9. Hong Kong   10. Indonesia
11. India   12. Kazakhstan

Lilywhite Gunners (pg 196)

1. Laurie Brown   2. Willie Young
3. Vic Groves   4. William Gallas
5. Sol Campbell   6. David Bentley
7. Jimmy Robertson
8. Pat Jennings

Turkish Delights (pg 198)

1. Fenerbahçe   2. Galatasaray
3a) İstanbul Başakşehir
b) Kayserispor   4. Fenerbahçe
5. İstanbul Başakşehir   6. Çaykur
Rizespor   7. Antalyaspor
8. Trabzonspor   9a) Galatasaray
b) Antalyaspor   10. Beşiktaş
11a) Fenerbahçe   b) Boluspor

Well I Never ... (pg 200)

1. Terry Mancini 2. Mathieu
Flamini 3. Bacary Sagna
4. Alan Miller 5. Paolo Vernazza
6. Ian Wright 7. David Hillier
8. Theo Walcott 9. Richard
Wright 10. Charlie George

The VIP Section (pg 202)

1. Alan Davies 2. Dido
3. John Lydon aka Johnny Rotten
4. Chris Lowe 5. Adrian Dunbar
6. Martin Kemp 7. Roger Daltrey
8. Bernie Winters 9. Frankie
Dettori 10. Nick Hornby

TRIVQUIZ

FROM ABBA TO ZAPPA, AMÉLIE TO ZULU, AND AGÜERO TO ZIDANE

NEW FOOTBALL AND POP CULTURE QUIZZES

EVERY DAY AT TRIVQUIZ.COM

 trivquiz.com   trivquiz   trivquiz   trivquizcomic